Red-Inked Retablos

Camino del Sol

A Latina and Latino Literary Series

Red-Inked Retablos

Rigoberto González

TUCSON

www.uapress.arizona.edu

Library of Congress Cataloging-in-Publication Data
González, Rigoberto.
Red-inked retablos / Rigoberto González.
p. cm. — (Camino del sol: a Latina and Latino literary series)
ISBN 978-0-8165-2135-7 (pbk. : alk. paper)
I. Title.
PS3557.O4695A6 2013
814'.54—dc23

2012031238

Publication of this book is made possible in part by the proceeds of a permanent endowment created with the assistance of a Challenge Grant from the National Endowment for the Humanities, a federal agency.

Manufactured in the United States of America on acid-free, archival-quality paper containing a minimum of 30% post-consumer waste and processed chlorine free.

18 17 16 15 14 13 6 5 4 3 2 1

Forever My Poet-Girl
Roxana Rivera

Y que en paz descansen,
Prima Verónica y Primo Daniel

If I could fly, I'd soar
above my neighborhood.
I'd spread my arms and
slice the space between
rooftops and ghetto-bird,
mapping all the little altars
flickering over blood
stained into concrete.
I'd soar off the ledge of a
helipad, going higher and higher
until the constellation of altars
turns into an image
I can understand.

—*Roxana Rivera, "Constellations"*

Contents

Foreword

When Butterflies Are Red: Mariposa Literary Activism

Rigoberto González's most recent visit to my home in early 2012 brought with it a familiar sense of comfort. As always, I looked forward to hosting my longtime friend, fellow critic, and, at heart, soul brother with whom I share an almost twenty-year kinship. Indeed, while Rigoberto's writing never fails to reveal another layer of his life to me, it is our curious familial bond that more often allows me to contemplate the multiple significances of his work. This visit was no exception. In tandem with his stay was a public reading of his 2011 poetry collection, *Black Blossoms*, at the tony downtown venue, the Roy and Edna Disney/CalArts Theater (REDCAT). Known as much for its support of avant garde work by fresh, new artists as for its wealthy and highly regarded patronage, the REDCAT is a leader in showcasing innovative visual, performing, and media arts in Los Angeles. Given González's rising profile among critics and artists alike, the invitation to read his work there seemed a natural fit. Thus, on the day of the big event, we headed out with great anticipation. Our arrival at the grand space, however, was not at all what we expected.

Perhaps we should have taken note when Rigoberto's name was not on the parking attendant's guest list. Perhaps we should have considered why his intended audience was crowded in the REDCAT hallway. Unfortunately, the reality that Rigoberto's reading would take place in a corner of the REDCAT coffee lounge instead of within one of its spacious state-of-the-art auditoriums did not occur to us until we entered. Although the event's gracious organizer and the audience's excitement buoyed the scene, as we settled into the few scattered couches and chairs and Rigoberto began to read, I found myself distracted by the quiet rooms across the way that remained closed to us. Like many other times in his life, I noted, González had found his way into the club, yet still remained just outside its VIP room.

I share this anecdote not to present Rigoberto González as the perennial underdog, but rather to introduce the ambiguous place he has held throughout much of his life. Being on the margin has frequently defined his existence. Rather than restrain him, however, this peculiar state of being has motivated him to master the art of communication. The REDCAT event demonstrated just that. Despite its awkward start, González's reading that afternoon went wonderfully. His words engaged; his jokes entertained. He even found ways of incorporating the whirling espresso maker into his performance. When he read a poem about Roxana Rivera, a young, deceased poet who shares a prominent place in both our hearts as well as in this book, he transcended his setting. The lounge became a screen depicting our tragic loss and the audience responded as if they were watching one of the venue's finest acts. Rivera's death, a very sad, personal event that both of us had experienced, was transformed into one that could be empathetically shared with others. It was inspiring to watch the audience moved by what had happened to someone we both treasured. Creating community through stories that touch on the imagination as much as they do the heart is in part what makes González such a powerful writer. His work has the ability to connect readers (and listeners) to subjects that might otherwise prove difficult to consider. His poetic language makes these issues feel urgent and, moreover, communal. Ironically, while the REDCAT's typical theatergoers might not have learned of his event that day, González created the kind of collective intellectual and emotional experience that the venue most widely promotes.

Another reason for beginning with this recent adventure is to help situate my role as González's commentator. As a married, heterosexual woman, I might initially appear an odd choice to open a book specifically focused on González's life as a gay Chicano. However, the messages about family, political camaraderie, and solidarity through language that reverberate throughout *Red-Inked Retablos* are the same ones that we have lived and shared as friends and colleagues. Our relationship is one that moves seamlessly between the love we feel as near-siblings, the commitment we share to advancing social justice within our community, and the passion we experience each time we read literature. This book takes its readers on González's journey for human connection, intellectual friendship, and passionate collectivity. Women play a significant role in all of these ventures. In fact, women have been integral to González's life. From the poignant loss of his mother in her early thirties, whose presence will likely always echo through all that he writes, to the aunts, cousins, and grandmother who attempted to assuage that loss, to his close female friends who still nurture him with care and kindness, Rigoberto is deeply embraced and loved by women.

Similarly, women are also professionally and politically significant. In their pioneer collection, *Gay Latino Studies: A Critical Reader* (Duke University Press, 2011), editors Michael Hames-García and Ernesto Javier Martínez note how the "lesbian feminist legacy of writing" has not only informed but also been "life sustaining" for many gay Chicano and Latino men who share similar political views and personal stories (2). As they explain, too often the divisions, imagined or real, between gay Latinos and lesbian Latinas are emphasized over the "interdependence" for a political race platform that includes them both. Instead, they suggest, there are "profound moments of cross-mentorship and collaboration" within the gay and lesbian Chicana/o and Latina/o communities as much as there are also distinct projects that each group engages in and respects the other for (2). *Red-Inked Retablos* illustrates González's sound belief in this perspective and, in addition, demonstrates how this camaraderie can extend beyond sexual orientation to include other writers whom he also believes require mentorship rather than rivalry. This is again where someone like Roxana enters as he explains in "Roxana's Melody." Roxana, other young poets González has advised, and Rigoberto himself have all learned from each other. Their growth is mutual, if not interdependent. After shepherding a group through their first national writers conference, he came to understand that "it was at that moment that I realized with a combination of fear and pride that this was my calling: looking out for the talent that I could nurture."

In fact, the publication of *Red-Inked Retablos* signals an important shift in González's role as a writer. The book arrives on the heels of a very prolific period in his life and during a time marked by great success despite the field's highly competitive nature. The strong reception of his work, which frequently explores dark themes and issues of sexuality not commonly found in mainstream literature, attests to its richness and allure. With thirteen books of poetry, fiction, and memoir under his belt, awards from the National Endowment for the Arts, the Guggenheim Memorial Foundation, the Poetry Society of America, the Before Columbus Foundation, and artist residencies that span the globe, González has become a recognizable writer of note. Similarly, his ten-year run as a columnist for *The El Paso Times* where he became the first national critic to exclusively review books by Chicana/o and Latina/o authors—along with a board position at the prestigious National Book Critics Circle and contributing editorships with various journals and literary magazines—have led to his taking on an increasingly significant role within literary criticism. *Red-Inked Retablos* thus does not set out to prove the merit of his writing, although you can be assured that you will find its lyricism powerful. Rather, this text is about marrying the poignant characterizations of exclusion and loss that run deep through much of his work with an outspoken advocacy for inclusion and recognition that he believes only literary activism can realize. González is a compelling presence within Chicana/o literature and criticism because he is able to offer frank discussions on the meaning of being a gay Chicano intellectual within environments that have had little space or appreciation for these identities. In *Red-Inked Retablos* he boldly claims a front-and-center position that demands acceptance of his sexuality amid a politicized Chicano subjectivity. As a groundbreaking text that combines personal history with a public call for literary activism, *Red-Inked Retablos* stands to date as his most expert meshing of desire, culture, community, and the powerful nature of language.

Red-Inked Retablos holds several meanings in its title. The collection masterfully combines various accounts from Rigoberto's personal life with reflections on writers who have influenced him and several speeches he has delivered at professional venues. In addition, the collection offers an in-depth meditation on the development of gay Chicano literature and the responsibilities of the Chicana/o writer. Although the topics might appear disparate, González neatly compiles them under the umbrella concept of "retablos," his literary take on a Mexican Catholic tradition meant to evoke devotional images, particularly those of patron saints. Like visual artists who use "ornamental structures . . . to construct interpretations that challenge, re-imagine, critique, or pay homage to the public expression of faith and desire, story and memory," González assembles retablos to illustrate the moments and people that led him to embrace a writing career. These retablos are Rigoberto's spiritual guideposts. Specifically, while the personal essays or "self-portraits" paint significant losses and the intense journey that ensues for love, acceptance, and a sense of belonging, the literary profiles or "studies" become the pillars of faith that fortify his search. Ultimately, they also give way to the public speeches that he delivers as testaments to his arrival as a mature writer and someone who has found salvation through his work.

Much like the blood-red paint that graphically decorates iconographic scenes in traditional Mexican retablos, reminding Catholic followers of what is at stake in their devotion, González employs a confessional writing style that draws his readers into action through the "passion and pain" that he bleeds onto the page. As he emphasizes in his decision to write *Red-Inked Retablos* as a work of creative nonfiction, bringing forward the "fury, fire, rage, outrage, and healing wound" of his memories with red ink is meant to vividly mark his experiences, both as a gay man and man of Mexican descent; the two inextricably linked. Most significantly, depicting himself in this manner, he hopes, will actualize not only his own life but will become a recovery project for many others.

Specifically, mariposas or butterflies are the subjects worshipped in *Red-Inked Retablos*. Well, perhaps not exactly worshipped because, as González reminds us, this is not a work about divine martyrs or saints who ultimately are impossible to emulate, but rather a work about human beings who seek contemplation and empathy. *Mariposa* is the term given, often hostilely, to gay men in Mexican culture. However, here, mariposas are openly studied and admired. Treasured for their perseverance and beauty. Respected for their tenacity. Throughout the book, Rigoberto tenderly teases out the various possibilities implicit in the butterfly trope. In particular, he notes the mariposa's ability for recollection. More than simply possessing the nature to change, he explains, a mariposa's "transformation is actually a transition. From one creature is born a different living being that bears the memory of its past life in its genes—the past is neither erased nor abandoned; the freedom of inhabiting a second manifestation of the self also represents a second chance at life." This second coming is what writing seems to best offer González and other mariposas. It is the opportunity to take hold of the pen and reject what has been said or written about them in favor of what they have honestly experienced. There is a rebirth that occurs when the mariposa is able to write his own story. The weight of memories that might have once brought despair is converted into a testament of strength, courage, and, above all, creativity.

Finding a place for mariposas to flourish is another significant theme in *Red-Inked Retablos*. González describes the many locations where he lands in search of a home. As a child, the agricultural desert town of Indio gives his family a purpose but leaves him acutely aware of what exists beyond its environs. With his mother gone, México becomes a site where he can remember her, but family members uncomfortable with who he is *not* often interrupt these moments of refuge. Stays in Washington, Ohio, Illinois, and Arizona ultimately lead to encounters with racism and homophobia despite the lucrative career opportunities they offer. And New York, where he finally settles, finding comfort among a large community of writers, still does not provide an altogether safe zone as his essay, "Orphans in the Terrorist World," reveals. While these geographical moves evince the liminal position González often occupies, they also underscore the multidimensional space he demands for himself and others. More specifically, as the militant gay Chicano voice he assumes in the speech, "Gay Brown Beret Suite," declares, "A need for visibility and space, for safety and dignity, and we *will* take to the damn streets if we have to!" Only a queer Chicano space where both identities are unequivocally welcomed will do.

The three genres that González employs—memoir, studies, speeches—serve as a trinity for the force he finds in language. In fact, he uses the word "trinity" in his concluding essay on a mariposa consciousness. Modeled after Chicana lesbian feminist Gloria Anzaldúa's essay, "La Conciencia de la Mestiza: Towards a New Consciousness," from her book, *Borderlands/La Frontera: The New Mestiza* (1987), Rigoberto's "Trinity" essay draws a visceral relationship to her, one that is not altogether surprising. Hames-García and Martínez also invoke Anzaldúa in their critical reader's introduction. Anzaldúa was among the earliest to adjoin the struggles of gay Chicanos and lesbian Chicanas and her commitment to building bridges of understanding and solidarity remains an exemplary paradigm. González acknowledges this fact in his remembrance to her in the study, "Beloved Jotoranos":

> The wisdom of this woman's vision allowed many of us to find a place in our community—to reconcile our sense of disorientation with and our affection for our very own tormentors—our families. Before Gloria, the intersection of ethnicity and sexuality, of Chicanismo + queerness = jotería, had yet to take shape as a theoretical framework. We lived it but we couldn't quite articulate it within the lines of our poetry, the plots in our stories, the strokes of our paintings. She gave order to the chaos of our multiple planes of existence.

The spirit of liberation that González celebrates becomes rather literal in the course of his discussion. Initially, he hints at Anzaldúa's presence when he lights a candle for her in his apartment and then more overtly as he tries to make sense of an awkward encounter with another gay Chicano as he imagines her using the meeting as an opportunity to educate the community, la familia. This is how González reinterprets religious devotion. Education, writing, and culture—working together instead of against one another—are the trinity that should bind the Chicana/o community together. In fact, nowhere is this premise more present than in the mariposa consciousness theory that González proposes.

Summoning forth the gay Chicano subject who has been shamed for his unintentional departures from Mexican masculinity, Rigoberto sets him(self) free as he recalls the protection that literacy offers the bookworm ("No one fucks with the reader"). This reassurance is followed up with a brief but exhaustive literary review that reveals to his mariposa subject that he is not alone. Specifically, the section "Mariposa Lit" provides a valuable summary of works, themes, and a multigenerational body of writers who give voice to the varied and thriving mariposa experience. Here, González advocates for the development of jotería studies and more mariposa scholars, emphasizing the need once again for activism and the validation of queer Chicano life. The essay concludes with a "mariposa prayer," a string of blessings to those mariposas seeking a higher education and to those who help them along the way. The prayer highlights the financial woes, the socializing and the friendships, the encouraging professors and the staff, the sisterhood with Chicanas, and ultimately, the carnal desire—to try, grow, and reach for the unknown.

González tells us that writing is "a way to recover what I no longer have." I would add that it is also a way for him to find what he never had. While reading Truman Capote's *Breakfast at Tiffany's*, he learned the art of reinvention through Capote's ephemeral character, Holly Golightly. In Truman Capote, he also found his first queer writer role model. Writing would become his exit strategy for a life that did not seem to want him and that he realized he could never fully enjoy. He notes, "I imagined Holly Golightly coming to the same conclusion because her dreams were much bigger than the space she was born into, and how she began to collect her new identity, word by word, until the time came for her to exist in another language." Writing provides González with a new language—the language of the mariposa—one that allows him to carve out a future entirely on his own terms. Moreover, it is a future that encompasses the unknown rather than the ill-fated destinies he witnessed around him. With this new language, he is also able to communicate with others. Arguably, *Red-Inked Retablos* collects a set of conversations had and conversations in the making. Not all of these conversations are fully realized as he discovers Andrés Montoya, Salvador Novo, and Thomas James regretfully after they have passed. Others are temporal, as his interactions with early risk-takers such as John Rechy and Richard Rodriguez demonstrate. Still others, however, are life-defining, for example, the mentorship he receives from Francisco X. Alarcón. The teachings of Chicana/o history and pride combined with the genuine and compassionate support that "Maestro Alarcón" provides González leave him with the most significant lesson he has come to uphold: "That is how a Chicano shapes a Chicano."

Red-Inked Retablos speaks volumes to its readers and it does so by both whispering lovingly and screaming defiantly. I hope that you will find all of its methods effective. Undoubtedly, this text will prove critical to several fields and is certain to advance much scholarship. Nevertheless, I also hope that you find it intimately touching and personal. *Red-Inked Retablos* is unapologetically revealing and Rigoberto has willingly exposed his life to illustrate the prospects implicit in mariposa literary activism. Butterflies are meant to be read and González is committed to make sure that they are. Or, as he might say if he was channeling his inner Holly Golightly, "Tough beans buddy, 'cause that's the way it's gonna be."

—Maythee Rojas, Associate Professor of Women's, Gender & Sexuality Studies, California State University, Long Beach

Acknowledgments

Thanks are due to the following publications in which some of these essays were published: *Cimarron Review*: "The Poet Ai: An Appreciation"; *Crab Orchard Review*: "The Truman Capote Aria"; *In the Grove*: "Andrés Montoya: The Ice Worker Still Sings"; and *Water-Stone Review*: "Orphans in the Terrorist World."

Part I of "Memory Lessons, Memory Lesions" appeared in *Family Trouble: Memoirists on the Hazards and Rewards of Revealing Family*; part II of that essay was delivered at the Association of Writers and Writing Programs Conference in Washington, DC, on February 3, 2011; part III first appeared in the Poetry Foundation Online Blog in November 2006.

"Beloved Jotoranos" appeared in *Who's Yer Daddy? Gay Writers Confront Their Forerunners*; "To the Writer, to the Activist, to the Citizen" was delivered as a keynote address at the Eighth Annual National Hispanic Writers Conference in Albuquerque, New Mexico; "The Gay Brown Beret Suite" was delivered as a keynote address at the Northeast Modern Language Association's Thirtieth Anniversary Conference in Boston, Massachusetts.

Red-Inked Retablos was supported by the Ford Foundation, JP Morgan Chase, the Andy Warhol Foundation for the Visual Arts, and Southwest Airlines through a grant from the National Association of Latino Arts and Culture (NALAC) Fund for the Arts. This grant enabled me to travel to Switzerland in the summer of 2007 for a one-month residency at Le Château Lavigny in Lausanne, where an early draft of this book was completed. I'd also like to thank the Trustees of The Frost Place for a residency at Robert Frost's farmhouse in Franconia, New Hampshire, during the summer of 2009, and to the Corporation of Yaddo for a timely residency during the summer of 2011. Eternal gratitude.

Poetry by Roxana Rivera is reprinted with the express permission of the Estate of Roxana Rivera.

Introduction
About Retablos, About Mariposa Memory

In the Mexican Catholic tradition, retablos are ornamental structures made of carved wood framing an oil painting of a devotional image, usually a patron saint. Mexican and Chicana/o artists have gestured toward these religious altar essentials to construct interpretations that challenge, re-imagine, critique, or pay homage to the public expression of faith and desire, story and memory. These are my versions of retablos, honoring ideals, people, occasions, and books—beloved muses that inspire my blood-ink on the page.

I was in my mid-twenties in the mid-1990s when I began writing personal essays. I had just graduated from a second creative writing program, earning a master's degree in fine arts with a concentration in fiction. My first creative writing degree was in poetry. Creative nonfiction was just beginning to surface as a popular third genre (and the category was as blurred then as it is now, encompassing everything from cultural criticism to memoir). Though I had never been enrolled in a creative nonfiction workshop, I gravitated toward this form that invited me to write about those subjects I was struggling with—my family, my sexuality, my past.

When I first revealed this interest to an older friend, also a writer, she scoffed at the idea. "What business does a twenty-something-year-old kid have writing his memoirs," she said. It was enough of a reprimand to keep me quiet about my labor for years, as I secretly wrote essay after essay, which I would later piece together into a book-length memoir. But not before I got permission through another conversation, when I admitted to a better friend that I hesitated bringing these essays to light because of that hurtful remark. His response: "Well thank goodness no one was around to tell Anne Frank that. She was fourteen." I am no Anne Frank, but that young woman's creative impulse gave me courage. I too had a vision of the world I wanted to commit to the page and, eventually, share.

Since publishing *Butterfly Boy: Memories of a Chicano Mariposa,* in

2006, I have had ample opportunities to flex that creative nonfiction muscle—from the lyrical essay to the scholarly essay and everything in between. The field and its popularity have grown considerably. What has been disappointing is observing that very few Chicano mariposas have added to the small body of creative nonfiction writings by queer Latinos. Chicana/Latina lesbians, on the other hand, have shaped an impressive intellectual, literary, and critical legacy.

Mariposa memory is not only important testimony about coming out and reconfiguring identity in relation to masculinity, culture, and religion, it is also about highlighting values such as education, shaping a sex-positive discourse, and exercising agency through a public voice. It is about making the queer experience a Chicano experience, and a Chicano experience a queer one. It is the affirmation of an intelligent, articulate, confident, politicized, and proud self.

This collection is divided into three sections, though it will become clear that the labels that separate them (self-portraits, studies, speeches) are simply different shades of red. Red as in blood, as in fury, fire, rage, outrage, and healing wound. These retablos commemorate passion and pain. Yet there is no martyr here—nor even a saint—only the honest illustration of human experience and thought. My purpose is not to claim Truth, but to provide perspective—mine—and invite a response to that flawed, imperfect point of view. In the end, that is what nonfiction writing, like a cherished retablo, does best: inspire contemplation.

Self-Portraits

The Truman Capote Aria

Television was one of our English teachers in the 1980s, the decade we had to adjust to our new home in the United States. Four branches of the González family lived together in a three-bedroom apartment in Thermal, California; the school-age generation included eight cousins, my younger brother Alex, and me. Each evening the ten of us would cram into the living room to watch one of the two snowy channels we were able to get without cable, while the adults, my paternal grandparents usually holding court, sat around the small dining room table in the kitchen to talk. The only time we came together was during *Buck Rogers* and *The Incredible Hulk*, when we'd laugh at Abuela invoking Jesús, María, y José at the transformation of Bill Bixby into the green beast. The Hulk frightened her because she thought it was a duende on steroids and therefore capable of terrorizing the streets in daytime. (Duendes were supposed to come around in the cover of dawn when their music and mischief was meant to occur without human witnesses, though every once in a while someone claimed an accidental sighting.) But otherwise it was made clear that because the grown-ups were discussing important matters in the kitchen, the women sipping coffee, the men nursing beers, the ten of us had to sit still and quiet in front of the television, which was kept at low volume.

The strategy for keeping the noise down worked for the most part, and only once or twice do I remember a disagreement breaking out over which of two competing programs to watch. These arguments were settled by Abuelo, who simply walked over the bodies splayed out across the floor and reached down to pull the plug from the socket, which added a dramatic flair to his dead-pan pronouncement: "Now go to sleep or I'll yank the cord out of the television too and then that's the end of that."

Because all ten of us were under fourteen, we were enrolled in the elementary school across the street. My older cousins resented being held back a year or two, but our parents were told that we had some catching up to do in terms of our English skills. I didn't care either way. At ten years of age, I liked school and my teachers and especially how my personal English tutor would show me new words, like "chores" and "chimney."

"*Shores* is something else," she said in response to my inability to pronounce the *ch* sound. "*Chores*," she explained further, "are what you do after school, after you're done with your homework."

I looked up at her, "You mean like watch television?"

She chuckled. "Not exactly. I mean what you do *before* you earn the right to watch television."

"Shower?" I said, explaining to her that because there were so many of us at home, all of us kids had to take our baths right after school, before the grown-ups got back from work.

"Okay . . ." she said, showing me her full set of teeth. "Then who mows the lawn and who cleans your room?"

We had no lawn. We had an old beat-up elevated porch in the front and a deserted lot in the back where the men parked the cars. My room was the living room, which I shared with nine others. In the mornings, all we had to do was pile up the blankets in the corner and then, like Abuelo always said, "That's the end of that."

"I see," my tutor said. And then she moved on quickly. "How about this word: 'chimney.'" I secretly hoped she wouldn't ask me to relate to that word either, since the only thing we had was a gas heater we used as a bench during television hours because we didn't all fit on the three-piece sofa set.

In reality, there really weren't that many "chores" to go around. The women swept, mopped, and did the laundry and the dishes. Abuelo cooked, mostly in an industrial-sized pot and mostly stew because it would feed the entire family. He was very territorial about his domain and whenever my aunts or my mother made a noble attempt at the stew, he had something to say about it. Once, he came over to peek under the lid and scoffed: "What the hell kind of meal is this? Where's the meat? It looks like you've got nothing but a piece of a dead man's nalgas swimming around in there."

All the rest of us had to do was not make a mess. Any display of sloppiness, no matter how small, was met with corporal punishment as an example to the rest of us. Besides, we didn't own too many things that could litter the house, like toys. And over time we didn't accumulate much else because our parents never had the money to spoil us with birthday or Christmas gifts.

Birthdays especially came and went without so much as a mention. I was devastated to find out that when I saw Abuela wiping off the inside of the front door it wasn't because she was helping prepare for my eleventh birthday—she was simply wiping off the grime that had accumulated on the wood. But my reward would come anyway, quite by chance. That afternoon she couldn't find her purse, so she had us turning every room upside down to find it, promising a prize to whoever found it first. I discovered it, lodged between the mattress and the wall. She gave me a dollar and I marched immediately to the local market to buy my birthday gift: a book of search word puzzles.

Thus the apartment with nineteen people was always neat and orderly. And to keep it quiet, there was the television. I do remember a small transistor radio that was kept on the windowsill above the sink, but I don't remember anyone ever turning it on, not while Abuelo was around anyway. So it simply sat there, snuggled among the row of plants like a pot that wouldn't flower. The only music we were subjected to was Abuelo's accordion, which he pulled out to impress company, followed by a selection of his Mexican folk records—Veracruz fandangos played with the harp and pirekuas from Michoacán sung to the violin in Purépecha, Abuela's native tongue. No mercy was shown to whatever youngster dared to laugh at the corny tunes. In fact, if anyone whined about having the television turned off, the volume on the stereo was turned up and the evening festivities would be deliberately extended into the night.

Thinking back on it, we weren't really missing anything spectacular. Television in the 1980s on the major networks was like cotton candy. The sitcoms were fantasy thirty-minute narratives in which the big family conflicts were disagreements over curfew or the right to take out the car. The story lines were so removed from my daily living experience that I simply thought this was how *Americans* lived, not *us*, the immigrant family from Zacapu, Michoacán. For us, the front door was always locked by eight o'clock and only the grown-up men had a right to sit behind the wheel. And no matter how much we stretched our frame of reference, the only way we could connect to *The Love Boat* was through a canoe ride everyone had to take to get from Pátzcuaro to the island of Janitzio in the middle of the great lake in our beloved homeland. But through the simplified conversations of these sitcoms on television we picked up an essential vocabulary.

"I beg your pardon?" was one of my favorite expressions, followed by: "Well, *I never*!"

These phrases, however, worked only on my cousins. I once blurted one out to my mother after she asked me to help her bring in the sheets from the clothesline and she whacked me on the side of the arm with the bag of clothespins because she thought I was being fresh.

My younger cousins exercised less imagination and simply adopted the catch phrases of the period, like Fonzie's "Heeeeeeey" in *Happy Days* with both thumbs turned up, or Arnold's "Wha'chu talkin' 'bout, Willis?" crowd-pleaser from the show *Diff'rent Strokes*. Somehow this last one didn't quite have the same effect in our household. When one of my cousins retorted with a "Wha'chu talkin' 'bout, Abuela?" the rest of us beat him down with the sofa cushions for sounding stupid.

For the next two years the routine did not change much, though tensions were running high and people were getting tired of the lack of privacy. But the television soldiered on loyally, even after the rabbit ear antenna was supplemented with aluminum foil and the plastic panel over the control buttons had to be fastened with electrical tape. It certainly did look like a casualty of war—and there were many raging within the walls of the house: two of my aunts had it out over the use of the washing machine, two of my cousins accused each other of losing the plastic top to the gallon of milk, someone wore someone else's sweater and stretched it, someone left the back door open, which let the flies in, and someone, Abuelo was determined to find out, had knocked over the salt shaker, which spilled and wasted all over the table. The excuses for conflict were small, and it was only a matter of time before the families, out of exhaustion and despair, dispersed.

Then one year each family went its own direction, but briefly, only to be brought back to my grandparents' apartment in Thermal after the death of my mother. We slipped comfortably into the old routines. Soon after, however, my grandparents decided not to live with the families of their three children. They had been so hurt by my father and his siblings leaving them the year before, that this time they would simply keep watch from a distance, in a decrepit house in front of the Thermal post office.

"Besides," Abuelo explained further, "we put in an application for government housing in Indio. They're sure to call us any day now."

No long after that, my aunt decided to return to México with her five children in tow. The three older ones had such a difficult time adjusting, they dropped out of school, but were still too young to get full-time jobs, so they roamed around town getting into trouble, especially the two males. My female cousin was kept locked up in the house because she had blossomed into a beautiful young woman, and her mother was afraid she would tempt one of the many young farmworkers camped out in the overcrowded all-male houses down the block. So off to México they went and those who stayed behind wished them well, though the adults gave each other knowing looks when reports came back from the border that one of the boys had run away, that the other had become an alcoholic, and that the girl had become pregnant out of wedlock.

In the meantime, there we were, my father and his two sons, my uncle, his wife, and their three children, reveling in the new spacious arrangement. And without my aunt's five children, I became the oldest of the kids, which immediately shifted the dynamics of who was in control of the television. I was.

My power was also based on the fact that I could stay awake so late. The adults no longer insisted the television be turned off by ten o'clock. As long as it was in low volume, no one said anything anymore. I would lie down near the set, close enough to reach up and turn it off when I was dozing off to sleep. This is how I ended up watching Johnny Carson's late-night talk show and then the old movies the local networks ran past eleven p.m. It took me awhile to catch on to Johnny Carson's humor—inside jokes that everyone in the studio audience seemed privy to. But I still felt left behind, like the times I heard the pre-recorded laugh tracks on sitcoms and could not understand what had been so funny about what had just been said. The late-night dramas were easier to grasp without the distraction of laughter.

My command of English improved so much that I was already reading entire books. I was particularly partial to murder mysteries and checked out Agatha Christie paperbacks from the library's bookmobile that made its way to my neighborhood on weekends. Excited by the genre, I also sought out mysteries when I leafed through the latest *TV Guide*. Weekend reruns of *Columbo* were my favorite, as were the old-school sleuth films featuring Sam Spade and Charlie Chan. Much later I realized that the local networks ran these old flicks because Thermal was part of the Coachella Valley, a cluster of desert towns that included Palm Springs, Palm Desert, and other golf course havens placed on the map by the many retirement communities that housed celebrities of times past. But my personal favorite was watching plot-driven stories that entertained me late into the night while everyone else was asleep. It was like having the house all to myself, something I pined for now that my mother was gone. During the day, when I wasn't in school, I had books to keep me entertained and isolated; at night, the television.

So it was with much anticipation that I awaited the showing of *Murder by Death*, a spoof on detective novels starring all of my favorite television and paperback heroes, but with a satirical spin: Sam Spade became Sam Diamond, Jane Marple became Jessica Marbles, Mr. Chan became Mr. Wang, and so forth. I even took a nap that afternoon to make sure I didn't fall asleep before the end of the movie. This was going to be the highlight of my fascination with murder mysteries and the exotic world of mansions and butlers. It would be like bringing my board game "Clue" to life; a game

I had convinced my father to buy me from the secondhand store but which I never got to play because half of the pieces were missing and the deck of cards was incomplete. I simply wiped the dust off the cover over the years and conserved it like a prized relic.

That night I sat down in front of the television and resolved to pay close attention. These TV mysteries were clever, distracting the viewer from the pertinent clues with red herrings and useless information. Once the movie got going I was thrilled with the setting, the quirky characterizations, and the jokes, like when Mr. Wang read the name and address plaque in front of the mansion: "Two Two Twain!" The movie was not quite politically correct, I would later learn, but in the meantime I was reveling in my ability to catch some of the humor. But then, once the odd assortment of detectives gathered at the dining table, a squat, funny-looking man came rolling in on a moveable chair and announced, "Good evening, ladies and gentlemen. I'm your host, Lionel Twain."

At thirteen, I didn't have to think too hard to realize this little man was a maricón, but glamorous somehow, like a pint-sized Liberace. His mannerisms, head gestures, even his voice were drenched in an affectation I admired. Now my favorite expressions were complete. "Well, *I never*!" I could say as I flung a hand to the back.

I had only seen representations of effeminate men on television movies, but not on television shows. In movies they were usually hairdressers or aerobics instructors with matching leg warmers and a headband, and they were as frail as moths. I could say the same in terms of stereotypical depictions of ethnic minorities: black people, Arnold and Willis notwithstanding, were usually the villains in cop shows, Asians and Mexicans were sweatshop workers and domestics. In fact, the only Asian actors I remember seeing on a frequent basis were the couple who spoke perfect English but who worked in a laundry facility in a Calgon detergent commercial. "Ancient Chinese secret," the young Asian man responded when the white client asked him how he left her clothes smelling so clean. And apart from Charo on *The Love Boat*, Ponch on *CHiPs*, and Speedy Gonzales on the Saturday morning cartoons, there was no substantial gesturing toward Spanish, let alone México.

I never questioned why these groups were so invisible, especially Mexicans. I suppose because I saw Mexicans every day. In fact, I had to turn to books and television to get away from them, to escape into a universe where conclusions and solutions were as certain as the end of the hour, or the final chapter of a book. In our household it was always the same old drawn-out story of poverty with no climactic plot-twist in sight.

So I turned my attention to this funny little man, who was a new type of homosexual. The actor's name was Truman Capote. I had never seen him in anything before, so I figured he was one of those showbiz folks from the 1960s, retired or dead by now. I didn't think much more about him until a few days later when there was a news brief interruption on the television. The news anchor announced that notable author Truman Capote had died in the Los Angeles home of Joanne Carson, ex-wife of Johnny Carson. No foul play was suspected.

I became dizzy. Those compressed sentences came loaded with information. Carson. Capote. Author. Foul play. It was as if all of my knowledge and interests had collided into a single moment that threatened to push me off the side of the earth. Suddenly this information I possessed held meaning, relevance, and context. It was like carrying around a compass all this time and coming across an occasion to actually use it. Indeed I felt oriented. I had a responsibility to find out more, to keep exploring now that I had a taste of something juicy. That Saturday I stood on the porch like a guard dog all morning, waiting for the bookmobile to turn the corner.

The librarian driver must have recognized the sight of a boy on a mission because I marched straight up to the big yellow van and demanded, "Do you have anything written by the actor Truman Capote?"

He chuckled, checked his box of index cards, and said, "Not here. But I can bring you something next week. What shall we start with? *Breakfast at Tiffany's*?" The title intrigued me so I went with that.

That same week another change occurred: my aunt had grown tired of being the sole caretaker of five kids and two grown men. There was that much more laundry to do, and more meals to serve, more dishes to wash. Indeed, all this extra work was placing stress on my uncle's marriage. I remember having that revelation the time we were all piled up in a station wagon on our way to visit relatives just across the border. My father was driving and my uncle rode shotgun. I sat between my aunt and my female cousin in the back seat. My brother Alex and the two youngest boys rode in the seat facing the back. We were sleepy, bored, and only a few miles from crossing the international line when my aunt and uncle got into an argument. I didn't pay much attention to the origin of the conflict, but true to my uncle's temperament, it escalated quickly.

"You know what?" my uncle said. "Just shut up."

"Why does it always have to end like this, with you shutting me up?" my aunt said. "I'm only trying to tell you that—"

"Shut up!" my uncle yelled, and he reached back to swat my aunt across the face.

"Hey," my father interrupted. "If that's how you want to behave in front of your children, that's your business. But I'm going to ask you not to do that in front of mine."

At the next stop, my uncle, filled with shame, ran out of the car, and we spent the next fifteen minutes following close by, my aunt with her face out the window, pleading, "Please get back in the car. Viejo, please get back in the car."

Not long after that incident, my father resorted to the most desperate of measures: he contacted Abuelo, who had since received that call from the government housing and was living in a two-bedroom apartment in Indio.

The thought of moving in with Abuelo again disheartened me, but I had no say in the matter. I had just turned thirteen. By now I had resigned myself to the fact that my choices had always been limited, like the two television stations, like the bookmobile—always samplings of a larger world. My father put it simply: we could move in with Abuelo, or go back to México.

"Why can't we just live by ourselves?" I asked, but the suggestion was silly. The three of us—my father, my brother, and me—living together like roommates, like in *Three's Company*? "Hey, everybody," my father would announce after coming home from harvesting grapes all day. "Let's go grab a bite at the Regal Beagle!"

The few times the three of us ever had meals together, we were continually struck by my mother's absence. One time a policeman approached us while we were dining at a pizzeria and he asked my father if that was his blue Mustang in the parking lot. We all froze, thinking that someone had crashed into it or that the wheels had been swiped, and then how the hell was my father supposed to get to work the next day. I could almost hear him blaming me for convincing him to take us out to eat at the dangerous downtown strip mall. It turned out the car had rolled back because my father had left it in gear and it was now sitting between two designated parking spaces. My father went to repark the car and then when he returned he refused to eat the pizza when it arrived, and I thought how sad it was that my father was so scared to go through life without my mother.

Moving back to México was not really an option either. I had grown accustomed to my American television, my American classroom, even my all-American bookmobile with its glorious collection of American voices. Once I got a mailing label on the *TV Guide* that had cut off the final letter of my first name, most likely because it was so long, but I adored the sound of it, Rigobert. I peeled it off carefully and saved it in a photo album. What would I do with all this American me in México?

My father had already made up his mind, but he sat down his sons to lay out the plan anyway. "Plus," he added, "Your grandparents have free cable where they live." I got an uneasy echo of the time Abuela came to Michoacán a few years before to tell us how much we would love the United States. "Plus, they feed you in school," she said, and she knew she had hit a vulnerable spot because we were going hungry in México, and all we ever got at our Mexican school were saltine crackers and hot sauce. And that wasn't even free.

"When are we moving?" my brother asked.

"It's better to do it before school starts," my father said.

Although I had acquired a vast amount of information, I had very few possessions. From the days when nineteen of us lived in one apartment, storage space was limited. Each family unit was designated a closet and that was the end of that. My mother had mastered the art of keeping all of our clothes underneath the bed. There were four long sheets of cardboard, which she could slide out depending on whose clothes she wanted access to. In addition to my clothes, all I could claim ownership to was a narrow bookshelf my parents had given to me when I won the fifth grade spelling bee. It was packed with books I bought at the Goodwill thrift store for a dime apiece, and my father assured me that there was a space for them at my grandparents' apartment. I didn't hold on to any of my toys, except for a bag of dominoes my brother borrowed to play war, propping them up on the floor like rows of soldiers and then knocking them down from a distance with a golf ball. We could have moved that minute if we needed to, but I suspected that was Abuelo's touch at work. He always had to have control over everything. Otherwise he wasn't happy. My brother and I braced ourselves for another few years of rules and restrictions, and of Abuelo lording over us his authority over the television.

Suddenly, I remembered the bookmobile and the copy of *Breakfast at Tiffany's* that awaited me on its next visit. I panicked, knowing Abuelo he would probably want us to relocate at the crack of dawn. But I worried unnecessarily because he wanted us there on a Sunday and the bookmobile always showed up on a Saturday.

"I'm moving tomorrow," I informed the librarian driver. "How will I bring this book back?"

"Oh, well, where are you moving to?" he asked.

"All the way to Indio," I said.

The librarian driver laughed. "That's even better," he said. "You know the main branch is located in Indio. Now we won't have to come to you anymore. You can come to us."

I marveled at the possibility. The only library I had ever known was the one in school, and it wasn't even its own building. It was a large room lined wall to wall with bookshelves and the librarian there was as controlling as Abuelo. Because there was no place to hide she stood over the check-out desk like a hawk, waiting to tell someone what they were doing wrong: "Don't turn the pages like that! Push the book all the way into the shelf! Don't just stand there looking lost; grab the book and sit down!"

If it weren't for the librarian driver, my opinion of book people would have been dramatically different.

"Our address is on the label on the back jacket," the librarian driver showed me. I thanked him and went off to read my book.

Reading *Breakfast at Tiffany's* was another revelation. First, I had to get over the fact that the funny little man in *Murder by Death* wasn't really the voice in the book. In fact, he wasn't anywhere to be found and I wondered how Truman Capote could do that, hide himself inside his words. Second, I must have missed something in the reading because I never found out who this Tiffany gal was and why Holly Golightly wanted to have breakfast at her place. But the part that really got to me was how Holly had reinvented herself, how she was wearing vocabulary and knowledge of the world to disguise her former identity—Lulamae from Tulip, Texas—and how she had left her past behind like a house too ugly to go back to or even admit she had once lived in at all.

I could relate to Holly. My cousins, after my aunt took them back to México, became resentful of me because I was reinventing myself in the United States. When we visited them in Mexicali, across the border, they called me gringo and humiliated me in front of their friends about how I loved gringo television and the gringo language. When we were still living in Thermal, I was subjected to a periodic tongue-lashing by my cousins because their mother held me up as an example. I was doing so well in school. I was learning English. But I was on their turf now, and there I was traitor.

"He's ashamed of being Mexican," one of my cousin's friends pointed out one time when we were out frolicking in the street and I refused to join in a game of soccer, not because I was ashamed, but because I knew I was a horrible player.

I really didn't understand why I wasn't allowed to fit in. Perhaps it was because I was ignorant of Mexican pop music or Mexican television personalities. But my cousins should have explained our situation to their friends—all those years with two stations in English and Abuelo's folk records. Or perhaps it was the way I spoke Spanish—the Michoacán inflections Abuela and my father still had were now undetectable in my voice, deliberately subdued because it was our cousins who ridiculed my funny-sounding Spanish. All this time I had been imitating *their* flat border Spanish.

But I didn't feel like a gringo. I still loved beans and tortilla and ate hot sauce as adventurously as my father. But I was also crazy about pizza and the hot dog, the first American food I remember eating when we crossed over. There really wasn't anything glaringly gringo about Thermal or even Indio, except that the young people preferred to speak English and, like my brother, listened to American heavy metal. Certainly my cousins shouldn't blame *me* because they dropped out of school. That was *their* choice. *I* was going to have an education. I had made my mind about it and knew that the way to succeed was by not being like my Mexican cousins. So I sought my future elsewhere.

I remembered the time my brother and I were watching an old Mexican movie, and there was a scene showing a young boy wandering around the square, his shoeshine kit under his arm. My brother turned to me in a moment of insight and said, "That's what we would've been doing now if we had never left Michoacán."

I thought about my cousins, one apprenticed to a mechanic, another to an electrician. *My* fate was school nine months of the year and the grape fields in the remaining three. Yet I knew I was simply biding my time. In five more years I would be an adult and I already knew I would leave this world behind because it didn't fulfill me. I imagined Holly Golightly coming to the same conclusion because her dreams were much bigger than the space she was born into, and how she began to collect her new identity, word by word, until the time came for her to exist in another language.

I was stunned after reading *Breakfast at Tiffany's*. Not in the way those surprise endings in the murder mysteries left me thinking about how the solution had eluded me. It was a different feeling altogether, as if the book was meant to guide *me*—the reader—to a discovery about myself. But the book was about Holly Golightly, *not me*. How, then . . .? Well, *I never!*

I became interested enough to seek out another book by Truman Capote. Because the gas and electric company had a bill payment office across from the library, I tagged along with Abuelo each time he went to pay. *In Cold Blood* was too thick for me to consider even touching, plus the title turned me off completely. It was about two murderers, and though I was no stranger to murder via Agatha Christie, I knew this wasn't written in the same manner. It took place in some farmhouse in the middle of nowhere; there was no baroness or retired English colonel to pull his pipe out of his mouth to raise his voice at Hercule Poirot with the firm but polite protest: "Why you unmitigated little bounder!"

There was, fortunately, a slimmer volume available at the library called *A Christmas Memory*, hardbound and in a little handy dandy box, like a Christmas gift. I had never seen such packaging for a book before so I knew this must be quite a special edition. I tilted the box and pried the book out with my fingernail. A musty scent was released into the air. I sniffed the cover, knocked on the spine, and then, to complete the five sensory connections, I consumed the story in one sitting.

This was a new experience also. It was almost like the other side of the Holly Golightly coin. Here, the narrator possessed an insatiable nostalgia for the people from the childhood he left behind: an elderly cousin who called him Buddy, Queenie the dog, and the unflappable Mr. Ha-Ha Jones, the saloon keeper. It was like looking at old family photographs and wanting to squeeze oneself between the bodies posing for the camera. It made me long for my childhood back in Michoacán, before the great migration to the United States, to that time when every morning had sound—the roosters crowing, the wagon wheels of the alfalfa cart spinning, the discarded bucket of water splashing on the cobblestone street. At the end of the story, when the narrator reads the sad news of his cousin's passing, I began to tear and feel almost embarrassed that a book could move me like this. I no longer thought of Truman Capote as that funny little man in *Murder by Death*, who had no pinkies and whose mother was a Roman Catholic and whose father was an Orthodox Jew. He was full of depth and humanity. How interesting this complexity in Truman Capote, he who was able to create narratives about reinvention through the glamor of privilege and about recollection through the amenities of the simple life. Indeed it was possible to slide from one landscape to another. And it was indeed possible to occupy both places at once. It was like being bilingual or bicultural.

I considered my grandparents, how they would sit around the table and reminisce about Michoacán. How they'd invoke the names of people and close the conversation with the certainty that they were probably dead. And whatever place they had left was no longer worth going back to because it was not the same place.

"They say they put up a fence around La Zarcita," Abuelo once said, recalling the multipurpose lake of our town, where women hand-washed clothes and boys learned to swim while young lovers picnicked within earshot on the grassy edge.

"Next thing they'll do is start charging admission," Abuela said.

"No," Abuelo said, his voice heavy with sadness. "It's not our Zacapu anymore."

But it *is*, I wanted to tell them, except that it now existed only in memory. I had *my* version of Zacapu, Michoacán, as well, and I still inhabited it when my new home in Indio, California, was letting me down.

In fact, lately, I kept going back frequently to Zacapu in my mind because I was having a so-so time adjusting to my new home and my new school. The housing project was crowded, noisy, dirty, and full of young men who dropped out of high school and joined the local gangs because there was no other choice, so they adopted the hairnets and the chinos, and patrolled the projects in the evenings. At night we could hear gunshots from the tougher neighboring housing project. We thanked our good fortune and remained safely inside the apartment, where we did have cable and a television with a remote control. But the novelty of these upgrades was overshadowed by the Spanish-language stations that my grandparents were tuned into day and night. The only English-language programs they watched were nature shows, which didn't interest me much. My brother and I had a smaller television set in the room we shared with our father, but it too was tuned to a single station most of the time, MTV, which had to be kept at low volume because Abuelo didn't want to hear heavy metal. I didn't care either way. I didn't have the streets and I quickly lost interest in the televisions I had no control over, but I still had my libraries—at school and downtown.

In junior high I couldn't get past the communal showers. I was a young man trying to find a footing in his sexuality, and seeing a bunch of other naked young men was knocking me off kilter. It surprised me how comfortable they were with their nudity, parading it around the locker room, no different, I concluded, than the dropouts who took ownership of the neighborhood when the sun went down. I was developing unfulfilled crushes that kept me sleepless at night and I resorted to the privacy of erotic fantasy, weaving lengthy implausible narratives in which one of these young men would come around and discover in himself the same passion and longing I had for him.

I withdrew into my most comfortable haven: books, and imitated their dignity—silent but bubbling with journeys and ideas, ready to communicate with the first person to take notice.

After school, I avoided the streets and stayed in my room, to the approval of Abuelo, who was complaining that my brother was getting himself into mischief out there. At school I kept myself quiet and away from any group. And despite the privilege of a free meal because of my family's low income, I avoided the cafeteria. I preferred to spend my lunch hour in the school library, running my fingers across the spines of books, cocking an eye at any provocative covers, and sitting strategically at the best spot in the room as I took stealthy glimpses at the good-looking boys in my grade while I pretended to read.

I was practicing my "come-hither" look—a seductive pose I had discovered in the back jacket of Truman Capote's *Other Voices, Other Rooms,* an old copy I stumbled upon at the Goodwill Thrift Store ten-cent bin. That funny little man, it turned out, was once a pretty little man, and I imagined him walking through the halls of his school like a peacock fanning all of his attention-seeking feathers. Even the masculine boys, I imagined, would have softened and succumbed to an unexpected desire. I was still not brave enough to attempt such a feat, but at least I had something else to aspire to: like my Holly Golightly exit from México, an exit from this body of a prison in which a homosexual was anxious to escape. I pictured my dramatic coming out, like those opera singers on those elaborate stages filmed for PBS. Everyone watched intently as the diva made her way to the center. With the spotlight directed at her, she turned to face the world, her back and shoulders lifted so that her lungs had room to expand and vibrate. And then her mouth opened wide as a canyon as she took in the first full breath. As she clasped her hands to keep her balance, she belted out the most glorious song, flooding the theater with the palpable throbbing of her blood.

Confessions of a Gay Catholic Boy

In May 2010 I made a special trip to México to baptize my nephew André. This was a trip made under duress because Lupe, my sister-in-law, insisted that her son be baptized before his first birthday. (Ten years before I went through the same pressure when I became my niece Halima's godfather.) I never quite understood this self-imposed urgency because, on both occasions, I noticed that the ages of the other children getting baptized varied from newborn to young adult. When I pointed this out, Lupe balked and said, "And it looks ridiculous to have a child walk himself to the holy water!" My brother just looked at me from the other end of the pew and shrugged.

In any case, the ceremony was brief and uneventful, except for that single moment during the candle-lighting ceremony, in which the godparents had to light the godchild's just-blessed candle with the holy candle located at the altar. We godparents had a group giggle at the realization that we were all too short to reach the holy flame. No one seemed to read much into the faux pas, but I did: as usual, I thought to myself, the church and its unattainable expectations.

The congregation continued to endure the sweltering heat for the sake of fulfilling the first of the seven holy sacraments. We zoned out through the sermon, sat and knelt through Mass, and stood for a few church hymns sung off-key. And then each family went home to party. At the González house, we ate a traditional Mexican meal, had a few beers, and called it a day. My brother and I sat around taking turns holding my nephew, who refused to relinquish the baby pope hat that was part of his christening outfit. Halima, in the meantime, went to her room to leaf through her catechism in preparation for her first communion.

We see these church obligations as cultural, not religious, because my brother and I are not church-goers, nor do we come from a church-going family. We were, however, subjected to baptism, confirmation, and first communion. The Catholic mandates aren't something we believe in, exactly, they're just something we do—like celebrating the Day of the Dead and Three Kings Day. It's the Mexican Catholic in us.

The Mexican Catholic in me comes out during those rare occasions I set foot in a church. Apart from baptisms and first communions, which require too much godparent participation, I actually enjoy the serenity of a simple Sunday Mass, from the reading of the scriptures to the chants and prayers that I recall with accuracy whenever I hear others utter them around me. The familiar experience comforts me.

I can't say that I ever left the church because I was never fully committed to its teachings, and, in some ways, Catholicism has been very good to me; its imagery and vocabulary—rosary, crucifix, genuflection—continue to inspire and inhabit my writing. I actually think it's a beautiful religion. Excepting the pedophile priests and the Vatican.

That opinion is not my opinion as a gay man, it's my opinion as a Mexican Catholic. Like many of my family members, I've grown increasingly disappointed in how the church has been chipping away at its own reputation, making chumps of all of us who continue to follow its tenets. It's not that we ever thought the church was perfect, it's just that we expected it to be a little more put together than the rest of us. It's the hypocrisy of it that bothers me the most. I mean, at every wedding, the priest, a man who is not allowed to marry, stands up to give the bride and the groom marriage counseling. And we let it slide, accepting it as a slight flaw in Catholic procedure. When our local priest drinks a little too much or is amusingly effeminate, no one points it out or does anything about it. But this child molestation epidemic (and the refusal of the Catholic leaders to address it) is something else altogether.

Interestingly enough, it's the church itself that's conflating homosexuality with pedophilia. To this day I've never heard any member of my family confuse the two, and it's not out of respect for me because I'm not out to anybody except to my brother and his wife. I suppose the church does this to make aberrations out of its fallen priests—to expel them because they never belonged in the first place.

I remember that during Halima's baptism classes (all parents and godparents are required to go through a series of religious teachings before a child can be baptized), the priest decided to go on a rampage against gay marriage. I sat, poker-faced, through the entire rant (the priest apparently, had come across some news item in the paper earlier that day) while my sister-in-law sat fuming. "What does gay marriage have to do with my baby's baptism?" she whispered to me.

I knew my sister-in-law was upset on my behalf, but she couldn't quite give it language because we were committing some sort of transgression: me, a gay man, had been chosen to be the godfather. It was clear the Catholic church didn't tolerate or welcome people like me, but there I was, not out of disrespect or even as some sort of activist gesture. I was doing it because I was Catholic and I saw a value in Catholicism that it apparently didn't see in me. I like to think my brother and sister-in-law appreciated that. It was very Catholic of me to be so forgiving.

As for the Vatican, only Abuela showed any respect for the pope. The rest of us rolled our eyes whenever we saw him on television all decked out in his fancy gown. When you're a working-class Mexican it's difficult not to be cynical and look at the pope as just another wealthy fat white man.

"I wouldn't kiss his ring," my uncle declared once. The pope was making his rounds through Latin America so there was plenty of footage on the Spanish-language stations.

"I'd suck it right off his finger," my cousin chimed in. "Pawn it."

And soon it was an all-out pope roast in the living room with Abuela becoming increasingly annoyed. Not even the popemobile could save him.

"Why doesn't he sell some of that gold in the Vatican and feed the hungry in Africa?" someone else suggested.

We had no problem spitting on the pope because he lived in some other part of the world and not in our poor neighborhoods. And so it was with a greater sense of betrayal that we now had reason to be suspicious of the priests among us, those within arm's reach of our children.

I found myself a bit dry-mouthed when I asked my brother if he knew if there was adult supervision at my niece's catechism classes. It made me feel I was unfairly persecuting all priests, just the way priests had been unfairly judging all gays as evil—only some of us are, and only when the occasion calls for it. But gays, we all knew, liked other men, not boys and girls. How much easier it seemed yesterday, before the scandals, when all one had to fear from the priest was a sermon preaching the horrors of premarital sex, masturbation, and homosexuality. Now, some of those same priests practiced something truly horrific. My anxiety about priests in general reminded me of something Sinéad O'Connor said on CNN: that she felt sorry for priests who now were afraid to be seen walking with children. Apparently, a few pedophile priests have destroyed our trust in all priests.

It saddens me, actually, because I believe I will see the fall of Catholicism in my lifetime. But it has to collapse, with its unattainable expectations of celibacy and abstinence and other cruel and inhuman repressions of human urges. And since homosexuality is equated with sex (I wish!), no wonder gays are especially despised by the church.

I've come to terms with Catholicism my own way, without feeling like I'm encroaching on a space I don't belong. I can count on one hand how many times I've actually prayed as an adult, and it's usually a prayer for my loved ones, like that time my sister-in-law almost died in childbirth. I believe in God, but not the policing and punitive one I have been told about all my life, the one my relatives always threatened us children with: "Don't do that, God is watching and he'll punish you!" If I'm entirely wrong I'll deal with it in the next life, not this one.

As a teenager I was terrified of God. He knew my secret and would one day cast me to hell for it. So I did the best I could to compensate for it. I recited my prayers and was determined to be a good gay kid, though like a true Catholic weakling I strayed at every corner. And after my mother died, in order to avoid believing that this was my punishment from God, I stopped praying altogether. Prayer was an admission of sin and guilt I no longer wanted to hold on to. If God wanted me, he was going to have to take me the way I was.

I have mixed feelings about those pedophile priests, however. To sympathize with them would be to disrespect their young and innocent victims. To demonize them would be to participate in the Catholic church's insidious method of accusation and persecution without perspective. The laws of man, indeed, are stickier than the laws of God. But then again, no one's asking me. But I do not want to belong to an institution that has been aware of its illness and refuses to heal itself. That is not *my* Catholicism. My Catholicism performs acts of charity, kindness, and compassion. Those values Christians in the United States purport to believe in, although their Republican politicians illustrate otherwise.

But for now there are certain things I can't shake out of my daily life, like lighting a votive candle whenever a writer I admire passes away, or slipping on a bracelet with the images of saints whenever I'm headed to the airport (it can't hurt!), or crossing myself as soon as I walk into church as a sign of reverence and affection for the architecture and sanctity of a church. I do own a Bible with my name embossed on the cover, but I only consult it as a reference tool and not as a spiritual guide.

Friends are constantly surprised by my position. They use as evidence of my atheism or disdain for religion the fact that I refuse to attend their weddings. I had to explain that I wasn't taking a political stance but my position was more cynical: the divorce rate. It makes the cost of my travel, my fierce outfit, and a gift a complete waste of money. If all else fails, I express resentment that marriage continues to be, despite minor triumphs here and there, a heterosexual privilege. Wedding invites have ceased to come my way since then. Thank God.

The last time I attended regular Mass I was startled by a number of things: the low number of attendees, how much I missed the ceremonies of Catholicism, and how antiquated the whole theater seemed whenever someone's cell phone rang. The church seemed stranded in some previous era while members of its congregation moved forward and moved on. In my family alone, many of us have officially left Catholicism to become born-again Christians, Mormons, and Jehovah's Witnesses.

But a few of us still hold on stubbornly. Like me, ironically. I'm still in love with the symbolism and metaphor of Catholicism, with the poetry of its litanies, with the drama of its martyrs, and the stories of its saints. I keep a rosary clinging to a photograph of my beloved mother who died in 1982. A wooden retablo hangs near my bed with a hand-painted image of Saint Francis. There's a statue of an angel in my bathroom and another on my writing desk, its frock decorated with small metal milagros. And the staple in every Mexican Catholic's household, la Virgen de Guadalupe, stands guard on top of my air conditioning unit—may it always keep working through those humid New York City summer days. I suppose Catholicism will never get rid of me because I will not get rid of it. I live and love among its artifacts—artistic reminders of what Catholicism stands for—hope and safety—not for what it has become.

Orphans in the Terrorist World

September 12. The date comes around each year, wearing the ugliest window on the calendar. As of 2001, it brings its equally grotesque older sibling, September 11. The two dates grate on me like subway trains shrieking to a halt on both sides of the platform. I'm forced to reckon with two days of remembrance back to back: 9/11 and 9/12, the date of my mother's death.

I still don't have the courage to talk openly about 9/11, or even write much about it. And for a year or two after the event it irritated me to no end to be asked by non–New Yorkers if I had been in the city during the terrorist attacks. The question is usually posed so nonchalantly, as if the answer could be given with the same casual tone. No, I was not in New York City on that fateful day, but in Seattle, calling or e-mailing everyone I knew in Manhattan, everyone I had left behind when I moved out of the city only six months before. Everyone I e-mailed eventually responded, dusty but unharmed. My only personal connection with the Twin Towers was that I went to browse the clothing boutiques in the underground mall once in a while, when I passed through. Because I was a middle manager for an after-school program in Brooklyn at the time, I had to attend meetings at the citywide coalition headquarters in the Wall Street district each month. But that personal connection became overshadowed by the patriotic agenda that exploited and manipulated a communal grief. There was very little room for "Me" when there was now a "We." I felt excluded every anniversary after that, so I simply refused to participate, making sure I hid out from the false sentimentality created by the American media.

This method of coping came easily for me, because by that time I had been practicing that same self-exile for many years. On September 12 I avoid any contact with family and friends. By now they have grown accustomed to my need for privacy and don't bother me about my yearly reclusive behavior. I descend into solitude for a day and ascend the next morning somehow refreshed, cleansed of a darkness that first took hold of me when

I was twelve years old. But each year, it comes back, this overwhelming clobbering of my spirit. And each year, I survive it.

In September 2002, after taking a year off to travel and heal after my last significant relationship ended, I was back living in Brooklyn, sharing a railroad apartment in Williamsburg with a musician whose middle name was Windchild and who was a good friend of my former boss (who was somewhat of a hippie herself) at the after-school program. I was now a visiting assistant professor at The New School in the Village and I didn't particularly care for my new neighborhood, which was young, bohemian, and very white. But the arrangement was temporary while I kept my eye out for an apartment in Manhattan, the Upper East Side specifically, because I liked how peaceful and clean it was—a far cry from the lively sidewalks of Williamsburg, where the loud energy distracted me from my work. I found solace in an unexpected invitation to a party on September 11 at a loft near the local riverbank, where young people gathered to watch the New York City skyline light up across the East River.

I had every intention of ensconcing myself for two days, but the hook of the party was: "Anything but 9/11." It was to be a response to the media overkill and political posturing that would surround the first anniversary of the event. And true to the theme, the conversations at the gathering were about anything *but* 9/11. Someone brought a large cooked fish, perhaps a salmon, which sat in the middle of the buffet table, getting picked to the bones as people, mostly artsy types, circulated through the room talking painting, poetry, film, and fashion. All the while, highballs and martinis completed the air of sophistication the hosts were aiming for. I gravitated toward the intimate clique of gay men generating the most witty banter and laughter. (*She asked me what I thought about her outfit. I told her it was out all right, now she just had to hope for a fit!*) It was a mostly Asian group, so I had no reservations about moving seamlessly into the conversation, and the group responded positively, if not politely, to my presence—I was one of only two Latinos at the party. Meanwhile, the industrial-sized martini shaker rattled in the background. Perhaps in anticipation of the following day, I drank myself stupid and stayed in bed weathering my hangover through most of September 12.

That particular year was a milestone for me. I had officially outlived my mother's age at the time of her death. She had been thirty-one, I had just turned thirty-two. In July of that year I wandered the city alone, trying to find a reason why I should live longer than my mother. I was not suicidal exactly, just unsure about what the stars expected of me. I had come this far, from Zacapu, Michoacán, to New York City, trying to elbow my way through the overcrowded halls of struggling artists. Would it pay off at the end, this sacrifice of living so far from home? Would it matter, this chosen profession: writing?

The next day, I walked through the streets of Manhattan. Facing the high-rise buildings was like facing the ocean, recognizing something grander than my small self. As I crossed paths with hundreds of other lives, I became comforted by the realization that there was no spotlight on me to scrutinize my actions. I was not the center of the world. I didn't have to make the right decisions, just the ones I could live with. That was the key phrase: "live with." The key word: "live." I had to live. That was all.

That same evening, after hours of stepping on the concrete sidewalks and not leaving behind a single footprint, I didn't want to go directly to my Brooklyn apartment, where I knew my roommate would be playing his keyboard and chasing his two Siamese cats, so I decided to check out the riverbank view from the ground.

I got off the L train at Bedford and walked toward the East River. People were headed in that direction but I didn't see any opening, just an abandoned shed. An older white-haired man with two dogs in tow was nearby so I simply asked how to get to the water.

"I'm going there too," he said in a thick accent. "Follow me."

He was Polish, like many older folk in the neighborhood who were being displaced by the younger hipster population. My landlady was Polish, as were the women at the laundromat and the workers at the deli. There were still signs in the windows in Polish and occasionally I heard it being hurled out from one side of the street to the other.

We got to the riverbank via that elusive hole in the fence and came upon other trespassers who were already comfortably seated facing the Manhattan skyline on cement blocks that resembled benches. I smelled pot but didn't think anything of it. This was, after all, the college-age crowd, the dreadlock-wearing white kids with trust funds and debit cards.

"It's beautiful," I declared, and became thankful for my luck. This was the most appropriate birthday gift—a view of the city I had fallen in love with from the moment I first arrived in 1998. From this angle it was postcard perfect, palpable because it was breathing back at me.

The old man stuck around, keeping an eye on his pets, and he struck up a conversation. I welcomed it, inspired into friendliness by the view. He told me he had arrived in New York in the 1950s, that he was later joined by his sister, with whom he still lived. He said it had been so difficult to fit in and to find a job at first because of his limited English, but that by some good fortune he was approached by a man who helped him out because he was also from the motherland.

The old man added: "So I asked him: 'How you know I'm Polish?' And he said to me, pointing down, 'The shoes! The shoes!'"

We both laughed, though I was unclear about how the shoes were the tell-tale sign of his nationality. In that moment, perhaps rendered vulnerable by my sense of gratitude, I imagined that this might be my first friend in Williamsburg, aside from my roommate, of course. So I didn't think anything of it when he turned to me and said, "You know you are a very handsome man."

I smiled, accepting the compliment, and that's when he leaned over and stuck his tongue in my mouth.

For a brief second I slipped into denial. I was no stranger to the kamikaze kiss, but the setting was usually a bar with men my age, well-groomed and balancing a cosmo in one hand. This man was as old as my grandfather and we were standing in mud while some deadbeats puffed on joints nearby. I wanted to tell him how sorry I was that he had sullied this night for me. It was my thirty-second birthday and today I was older than my dead mother. Reaching this age was like receiving permission to move on and live. In my twenties I was convinced I wouldn't make it, and more than once I planned my exit to the sharpest detail—a razor blade across my right wrist. I went as far as testing the path of the cut, a stupid exercise that left scars on my flesh. I wanted to accuse him of giving us homosexuals a bad name, of betraying my trust, and offending me when all I wanted was his guidance—his friendship even.

I stared him down. By the way he took a step back he seemed to understand that I had not been flirting with him this entire time. He looked afraid suddenly, and fragile. So I simply smiled apologetically and thanked him for showing me to the riverbank. As I walked away I had to laugh at how silly the whole exchange had been. Once I got to the street, I laughed out loud and realized then that this awkward pass from an old man would keep me from plummeting into depression that night.

I slept well and peacefully.

I finally left Williamsburg in the spring of 2003 and moved into a one-bedroom Manhattan apartment on East 88th Street and York, on the opposite side of the East River. This was also my first encounter with the dreaded Housing Board process, even though I was renting the place from my accountant. Still, it was worth the trouble and the countless paperwork, which included three reference letters, a letter from my previous landlord, which I forged, a copy of my job contract with salary statement, and a notarized letter from my bank revealing information about my personal accounts.

This was the first time I was living in New York without a roommate, which meant that the hardwood floors and the view of gardens and greenhouses were going to cost me dearly, but for a year I pulled it off. The other benefit of my address was that my favorite gay bar, the O.W. (as in Oscar Wilde), was just a short cab ride away on 58th. For months I collected cab receipts that were oddly around the same amount because I rode those same thirty blocks many times after last call.

The Upper East Side, which every New Yorker who doesn't live there calls boring, has a quaint neighborhood feel east of Lexington Avenue. After a few short months I earned the right to be remembered by the people who saw me often at the cleaners, the deli, the local food market Gristedes, the post office, and Maz Mezcal, the Mexican restaurant on 86th that served the best mole poblano in Manhattan. The subway line was so removed from where I lived that foot traffic was never dense, so I was able to adopt a new exercise routine: walking down 1st Avenue all the way to Murray Hill, sometimes further south, and then back up again. Thus my days went like this: mornings teaching at the New School, mid-days working at the computer, afternoons hoofing it on the concrete treadmill, and evenings drinking at the bar.

When September rolled around, I knew what I wanted to do on the eleventh: hide out at the Town House, the gay bar across the street from the O.W. When I felt like being left alone I went to this bar because it was frequented by older gay men, most of whom were classy and respectful. They'd been around and had seen most of it, so they could spot a guy looking for action but also anyone simply walking in for a relaxing happy hour cocktail.

That was me on September 11.

I detected a conversation about 9/11 at the bar upstairs. A white gentleman kept declaring in his broken English that he "could not believe it, the buildings, they fall!" The bartender was wearing a tight-fitted shirt on which the American flag, in colorful sequins, covered the entire front side. I quickly made my way to the downstairs lounge. It was quieter, the light more subdued, and not very populated at the moment. I pressed myself into the corner and ordered a dirty Absolut martini. I appreciated that the bartender wasn't chatty or anxious to reveal where he was or what he was doing the hour the towers collapsed. I had seen those unforgettable images on the television back in Seattle, where, at the time, I was visiting my cousin. I had no television at my apartment so I rushed over to his house to keep abreast of the situation. Shortly before the collapse, cameras had inadvertently recorded the sight of bodies falling—jumpers who had succumbed to hopelessness. I was sitting on the couch when I heard my cousin talking. His voice startled me back to consciousness. I had fainted.

It wasn't watching the footage that had caused it, it was flashing back to a tragedy I had witnessed only days after I moved to New York City in 1998. My then-partner had recommended that I walk around the neighborhood at 62nd Street between Lexington and 3rd Avenue to get to know the place. I had been timid about exploring, awestruck by the sheer size of the buildings around me, by the numbers of people on the sidewalks. I had never lived in a big city before.

Eventually I took his advice. I wandered the streets in the area, always heading west because going to Central Park gave me a purpose: to find a bench to sit on and read. I was already a little apprehensive about spending my first winter in the city, so I was not deceived by how mild the weather was that day, December 8, to be exact. With a coat, a hat, and a pair of gloves in my bag, I was ready for anything, I thought. On my way back from the park, I was meandering along Madison when all of a sudden something dropped from the sky. Because I had seen restaurant workers toss large bags of garbage onto the sidewalks I thought that's what it was. It wasn't.

A woman had jumped. I zoomed in on her yellow socks, soiled at the heels. Pedestrians all around me stopped and stared. Chauffeurs leaning against their town cars spoke into their cell phones. I turned around, headed straight for home, and waited until I locked the door behind me to cry, though I wasn't sure what I was crying about. I felt a sadness I didn't understand. What kind of place had I just moved to? I imagined that once the body was removed and the sidewalk cleaned, the flow of foot and vehicle traffic would continue unaffected by the soul that had caused little more than a pause in the system. I cried into my partner's arms when he got home after work, and I told him I never wanted to speak of it again, though it took me months to recover. When the 9/11 footage appeared on the screen three years later, causing me to black out for a minute, I realized I had only repressed that memory.

The bartender downstairs at the O.W. was more preoccupied with his new cell phone than giving any patron much attention. On any other night I might have been indignant, but not on that night. I appreciated my invisibility. But as I sipped my drink, letting the olives tumble up the side of the glass toward my lips, I felt I was being watched. Behind me, a white guy about my age, but bald and with a hairy chest, walked past, and then walked past again, as if sizing me up from different angles. I turned around and watched him sit at one of the small vinyl seats in the corner of the room. He was attractive, with a shadow of a beard on his face that had always been a weakness for me. He smiled. In an instant I left the bar to join him. *What the hell,* I thought.

We struck up a superficial conversation about this and that, made jokes and flirted.

"Yes, I'm a professor at The New School."

"Oh, really, I went to NYU."

"It's kind of quiet tonight, isn't it?"

"Well, it is the day it is."

He reached over to touch my cheek; I reached over to feel his hand. The chemistry was unmistakable, I convinced myself. I didn't even flinch when he made the odd request to look at my socks. I lifted the cuffs of my pants, and he reached down to pull them up.

"I have a thing for dress socks," he said. *Whatever floats your boat, buddy,* I thought.

"What are you thinking?" he asked.

I knew the answer to this question, which was clearly an invitation for me to make the first move, so I said boldly, "I'm thinking: Why aren't we in a cab on our way to my place?"

"Actually," he said, "I was hoping to circulate a little more this evening."

The rejection hit me like a sucker punch. He must have seen my eyes widen, my pride drop to the ground, taking my face with it, because he quickly added, "It's not what you think. Look, I can't explain it to you now, but I want to. Can I call you tomorrow? What time do you usually get up?"

"Sure. I'm up by nine."

I appreciated his pity, so I wrote down my number on a napkin and gave it to him, expecting never to hear from him again. I said my quick good-bye and a few minutes later I was in the back seat of a taxi. What a surprise to actually get a call from him at nine o'clock the next morning.

"I'd like to see you tonight," he said. "I'll give you a call at noon."

He called right on time, letting me know he would call me again at three. He did, and we made plans to meet at my place at six. I didn't ask him about his frequent phone calls, partly because I was distracted by my own sense of disorientation because it was September 12, the anniversary of my mother's death. I thought it particularly tacky to have a boyfriend over on that day—something I've never done before—but I had been left dissatisfied the previous night and had spent all day warding off a depression about my mother with the anticipation of my new beau's arrival. I distracted myself from the anxiety of his pending arrival by sitting at my desk and working on an essay about my mother.

While I typed, I kept looking at the altar I'd set up for her: a sepia photograph of Avelina Alcalá at nineteen, a rosary draped over it, a few lighted candles, and a Day of the Dead skull. These objects were set up to trigger my inspiration, but I made it a point to hide them away before the boyfriend arrived. I didn't want to have to explain them or the fact that I was hooking up on such a significant day.

He arrived on time, at exactly six o'clock. I buzzed him in and as he made his way up to the second floor I took one quick glance around to make sure everything was perfect. A bottle of wine. *Check.* Condoms in the drawer. *Check.* A sheet to spread on the futon couch in the living room. *Check.* He knocked, I let him in, and within minutes we were snuggling on the couch.

"Take it easy," he said, pushing me politely away.

I shook my head. "I don't get it. I thought this was why you came over."

"It is, but can we take it a little slow?"

I had to admit that was a new one—a phrase I had never heard from another man. But I complied. "Okay." I got up to pour some wine, then handed him a glass. "What would you like to talk about?"

"I don't know. Well, what did you do all day?"

"I wrote. I'm working on an essay."

"What about?"

"Oh, my mother," I admitted, and immediately felt a knot in my throat.

"Is she still alive?"

I was disarmed by the question. I took a sip of wine. "No."

"I'm sorry. When did she pass?"

At this point something in me crumbled. Whatever libido had me humoring this guy's strange courtship habits fell apart and I felt naked, but not in a sexy way. I turned to him. "Can I be perfectly honest with you?"

"Of course."

We had now agreed to be so open with each other that I could see the child this man once was in the expression on his face: "Today is the anniversary of my mother's death. She died twenty-one years ago. The reason I was at the Town House last night is that I prefer to be alone during this time of year. When I met you I figured I might as well get laid while I was out there drowning my sorrow in a martini glass. Now I feel like an asshole because this is the most disrespectful thing I could have done in memory of my mother."

Suddenly his eyes bulged. He put down the glass to rub his hands against his temples.

"What's the matter?" I said.

"You're not going to believe this," he said. "Yesterday I got a call from my father in Florida. My mother died, and I couldn't get a flight until tomorrow, so I went off to the Town House last night to distract myself, and all day today I had friends keeping me company in three-hour shifts, which is why I kept calling you back—you're my six o'clock—since I had just met you I wanted to make sure you didn't back out. And now I'm here and your mother is dead and my mother is dead and it's freaking me out. What do you think this all means?"

I put my glass down as well and held his hand. "Maybe it just means that our mothers are watching out for us. Knowing you were coming by this evening got me through the saddest day of my year, and I'm here to show you that it's possible to be without a mother for twenty-one years."

"Maybe," he said. And we left it at that.

We chatted for another hour like a pair of cousins and then he was on his way to meet his nine o'clock appointment. We kissed good-bye and promised to be in touch once he returned from Florida, but we never did. It was as if this day was all we were going to have, all that we were meant to have, we two gay men, orphans in the terrorist world, who would roam the rest of our days without mothers.

My appointment at The New School came to an end in the summer of 2004. Without a job in the city, there was no way for me to afford my Upper East Side apartment, so I decided to leave New York for a spell. I accepted a one-year university appointment in Ohio and in August I moved to Toledo, where I expected nothing more exciting than the inevitable winter that was going to come my way. After a brief tour of the campus and town, I knew I was right. Because I had no car I walked everywhere; occasionally a Good Samaritan would pull over and offer me a ride. Twice this happened while I was out on a power walk, as if watching someone exercise on the street were an unusual sight.

There were a few gay bars but none within walking distance, and though people were polite, there was something impenetrable about these Midwesterners, as if they could detect my many levels of foreignness: Chicano, New Yorker, gay. That didn't stop me though from appreciating the pretty corn-fed college boys at the local coffee shop, where I sat for hours grading papers or reading, and then glancing up at the more attractive men who came in to order a vanilla latté to go.

In early September, I was sitting at a table reading and ogling, when I noticed a husky brown-haired man sit a few tables away. When he smiled I smiled back and didn't mistake it for flirting because I thought that such an explicit activity would probably never happen in a place where people were proudly Catholic or Christian. This was an election year and already the propaganda was furious with declarations of loyalty to a certain political party that was running on a religious platform. Ohio, the powerful swing state that year, was receiving much attention.

But all the political dramas would come later. In the meantime I sat there reading and sipping my coffee. When I looked up again I noticed that the guy had moved one table closer to me. He smiled again. *How odd*, I thought. *And ballsy*. I figured this would probably be the closest I ever got to action in this state so I decided to pursue it. I smiled back. He motioned to ask permission to come over to my table and I nodded, thrilled at how easy this was becoming.

"Howdy," he said.

"Howdy."

"You're not from around here," he said.

"No."

"Just visiting?"

"Sort of. For the year."

"I'm from here, but I'm visiting also," he said. "Visiting my parents. They still live here."

I'm not sure if it was the Midwestern method, but the chit-chat lasted a good hour or so before we got into anything remotely resembling a flirtation. But we got there, and an hour after that we were romping around on my futon couch. I'm also not sure if this too was the Midwestern method but he was loud and the walls in that building were thin, and I knew that if there had been any speculation about my sexuality it was now confirmed.

We had a good time, but that was all. He told me he loved Florida and had a boyfriend back there waiting for him, but that they had an understanding about these things. I didn't judge; I had just benefited from the arrangement.

"Can I come back?" he asked.

I laughed. "Anytime."

"How about this Saturday?"

A chill ran down my spine. Saturday was September 12. I had almost cheapened that day last year. Would I ruin it on this one?

"Sure." I couldn't resist. And a few days later there he was in my apartment. We had sex, we drank wine, and he snored all night. I didn't feel guilty at all that this was happening on the anniversary of my mother's death, though I kept thinking about her.

The next morning we said our good-byes. My lover was off to Florida and to his boyfriend, and I was staying behind to teach Latino literature and twentieth-century American poetry to a group of college kids who were mostly attending the university to become schoolteachers. I didn't expect to hear from him again but he called a few days later.

"Hey," he said.

"Hey. Are you calling from Florida?"

"No," he said, sounding sad.

"What's the matter?"

"I had to postpone my return a few days. Plus there's some hurricane hitting the area so I may end up staying longer. I'd like to see you again."

"Sure," I said. "Anytime."

"You know. I just want to let you know that I really like you. Seeing you again doesn't make this seem dirty, not like a one-night stand or something. And you've heard me snore, for Christ's sake, so it's more like intimacy what we've got going on."

I had to roll my eyes at that, thinking that this guy was just trying to keep from feeling guilty that he was cheating on his significant other. But I played along.

"So when are you coming by?" I asked.

"I'm parked out front, actually."

I rushed to the window. Indeed he was parked outside. "You weirdo. What the hell's the matter with you?"

"I needed some time to think. Can I come up now?"

"Come on up," I said.

We snuggled on the couch. He seemed distracted and because I was his surrogate boyfriend while he was away from Florida, I felt compelled to own up to the responsibility.

"So talk to me," I said. "What's going on?"

I was completely unprepared for the tears, which he wiped off quickly.

"What?" I asked, genuine concern in my voice this time.

"I haven't told you the reason I'm here. I actually came down here to bury my mom." My face flushed. "She was in bad shape and slipping away, so I made it down here in time to watch her die. She finally passed when I saw her at the hospital the night after you and I made love. I was at the foot of the bed. My sister and my dad were on either side of her. When she finally died her body jerked up and I felt her go through me. It was the most intense feeling I've ever felt and I realized that it was a gift, or a blessing, to let me know she thought it was okay that I was gay and living with another man in Florida, that she loved me no matter what."

I thought it impossible that this was happening again. Was I to be the provider of solace to gay men who were about to step into the uncertain, motherless world I had inhabited for so many years? Or maybe I was misreading some message, perhaps from my mother? Was she telling me to stop picking up strangers? Or was she telling me it was okay that I was gay and exercising my sexuality?

I decided not to reveal any of this to Mr. Florida. What he told me had been beautiful and it was his moment of bliss, so I left it at that. We didn't have sex that evening, but he did spend the night. I set the alarm while he called his father to let him know he was staying with a friend, that he needed some privacy, and that he'd be there bright and early, in time for the services. He pressed his body against mine and I held him. When he broke down in tears I cried with him.

The next morning he said he would be back to Toledo sometime in the near future, and that he would give me a call. He told me that there was something quite special about me. "I mean it," he said, "that's not just a line."

I smiled and let him leave, certain that I would never see him again. Whatever he needed from me he had already taken. Whatever he had to give me had already been offered up. I closed the door and proceeded to put up the altar for my mother. I had become so distracted that week that I had neglected to set it up in time. Somehow I knew my mother was fine with that.

Easter Rock

1983

My family took to Easter much like it took to Halloween because even though we were a non-church-going Day-of-the-Dead–celebrating immigrant family from Michoacán, we wanted to fit in. We nailed down the basics—plastic Easter eggs filled with candy, marshmallow Peeps, and chocolates shaped like bunnies—and then, once we renamed the religious holiday "el día de la coneja" (Day of the Rabbit), we filled in the rest of the blanks the González way. That meant buying braids of intestines, cured sirloin, and beer, oiling the shotguns, and heading out to the middle of the southern California desert, where the men in our family got drunk and lit the grill with gasoline siphoned from one of their cars.

Because this was what my family did I learned to enjoy it, though I knew Americans celebrated Easter much differently—I had seen them do so many times on television with their delicately decorated eggs and baskets brimming with curly seaweed grass. Still, I liked the freedom of the desert, the way the adults clustered around the food and laughed while the kids were allowed to explore unsupervised. We'd climb trees and boulders, fall and skin our knees, pick wildflowers, and above all else we'd keep our eyes open for snakes.

"And don't scare it away if you find one," Abuelo called out. "That's lunch!"

I remember these outings as the only times we actually looked like a happy family and I always regretted that we were so far off the main roads that not a single car passed by to take note of our harmony. How unfortunate that our neighbors had such a one-sided view of us: nineteen people squeezed into a tiny apartment in which ten kids ran out of the house fleeing the belt and nine adults argued on the porch until someone threw a half-consumed beer at someone else and the can would stay on the ground growing warm for hours until someone had sense enough to pick it up.

But at the Easter Sunday outing no one got a beer thrown at them, not even in jest. Instead, the radio played and we'd laugh at Abuelo dancing with a piece of meat dangling from the tongs. And then, once the men got a few drinks in them, they walked over to the car and popped open the trunk.

On one such Easter celebration, from the corner of my eye I saw my uncle pull out the burlap sack containing the shotguns and that's when my anxiety began. All week my uncle kept promising my older cousins that this year was their turn to shoot and each time he mentioned it my cousins would beam. I wasn't too keen on the idea so I didn't react. My father must have misunderstood my apathy for wistfulness because on one occasion he walked up behind me and said, "Don't worry, I'll make sure you get your turn too."

I was too stunned to correct him so when the sack came out of the trunk, I hoped they would forget it was our turn to shoot, but my cousins hadn't forgotten. As soon as they noticed the guns being pulled out they ran over, hollering, and left me sitting alone on a rock.

What was it about guns that intrigued the men in my family? I didn't understand it. I had grown up around them—rifles for hunting deer, BB guns for pigeons and doves. I was more interested in the shells, big plastic ones with a copper base, round like a penny, and metal ones that I could use to whistle. One time I pocketed so many my shorts kept sliding down my hips and my father made me throw them out before I climbed back into the car.

The truth was: guns frightened me. Their weight, their bang, their boom, the ricochet that left my ears ringing, the harm they did to the birds whose eyes looked so human with the lids closed. That was my job on those hunting trips. I had to pick them off the ground, dig for them in the brush, the red wound disrupting the smooth surface of feathers and down. Sometimes my uncle would pluck them on the spot and their naked little bodies of pimpled skin looked violated, not edible at all.

I had never killed a living thing, except for an injured hummingbird once, and by accident, because I thought I was saving its life by pulling out that funny-looking twig sticking out of its beak. As soon as I figured out it was its tongue I burst into tears and prayed for forgiveness over its tiny grave for a month.

But neither did I want to shoot a gun. Guns were not pretty or graceful or pleasant, they were vulgar things without much imagination: they caused damage or death and nothing else.

Because the younger kids were not allowed to shoot (they would have to wait to be at least twelve years old like me) they were enlisted to collect the empty cans and line them up at the clearing. I made the mistake of picking a can up. My father quickly corrected me by grabbing it out of my hands and throwing it back.

I don't know what I was hoping would happen, but as soon as the action started I made no effort to fight to be the first to shoot or to even stand close to my uncle as he demonstrated the safe way to load, hold, and shoot. I wanted to say something clever like, *Wouldn't it be safest not to even touch the gun?* but I pictured my uncle giving me the knuckle on the head. Instead, I just kept quiet, wishing that somehow I would become invisible.

My fifteen-year-old cousin went first. He stepped up to the firing range like he had been born for this and made a big show of taking aim, deliberately drawing out the moment to the point that even his mother called out, "Shoot the damn thing before I fall asleep already!" He shot his two rounds. Everyone clapped and he bowed. And then another cousin stepped up, but he was a big lug with a man's body at thirteen, so no one expected anything less than a seasoned performance. When my turn came, I sensed the enthusiasm plummet. The rifle was heavier than I thought and when I almost dropped it my uncle said, "That was my fault," and I knew no one had believed him, especially not my father who looked like he was wishing for the miracle of instantaneous testosterone.

When my uncle stood close behind me, positioning my stance, he whispered into my ear, "Don't fuck this up. Your father's watching." And I knew then that I would indeed fuck this up. I fucked it up so badly because when I shot once then twice, the rounds didn't even make the same noise they made when my cousins pulled the trigger. Or at least it didn't sound like it to me. I couldn't even tell if they had hit the ground or if the shots had raised dust or anything because I didn't see very clearly, even with my eyes wide open. The whole thing was anti-climactic: our audience had seen it done twice before and done better. To add insult to injury, no one clapped and my father simply turned around and reached into the cooler for another beer.

My oldest cousin broke the spell by shouting out that it was his turn again, but by now everyone had lost interest and had moved onto other activities. I relinquished the rifle and it felt like I had just handed over whatever it was that my father had wanted me to be. And so I slipped away, watching the fun taking place without me. I sat back on my rock and recalled every other time I had disappointed my father. One moment stood out, though that Easter Sunday had already risen to the top three. Once we were visiting family across the border and I bowed out of a game of hide-and-seek because there were too many creepy places to hide in that badly lit street. I was called a chicken but didn't think much of it, until I got bored watching television inside the house all by myself so I decided to go back out. I saw my father sitting on the sidewalk with a few of the boys, and I thought it would be funny to sneak up and scare them with a nicely timed scream. But as I approached them I caught a snippet of their conversation.

"Why is your son so afraid of everything?" one of the boys asked.

"Like what?" my father said.

"Of *everything*. Like, of the dark."

"Well, he was raised differently. In the North. There are plenty of lights up there."

I wasn't sure what hurt me more: my father's shame or my own at having to witness my father making up an excuse that no one really believed. At that moment I changed my mind about sneaking up on them. I slunk back into the house and tried to sit in the living room with the television off. Eventually, predictably, I got scared of the dark and turned the light on.

Just as easily as I slipped away I slipped back into the Easter Sunday party. We had our meal, drank orange soda, and set off to look for the Easter eggs. This year we didn't have enough of the plastic ones, so my aunt fashioned a bunch out of aluminum foil. So many other activities took place that no one mentioned the disaster with the rifle, and I would have forgotten it myself except that it all flushed back into my face each time I saw my father.

Once we had found enough eggs, we sat around wherever we could find shade to eat the candy. I sat next to a boulder and picked the nettles off the cuffs of my pants. When my father came up to me I didn't even look up. Whatever reprimand I was going to get I would take with my head down.

"I found something too," he said.

The gentleness in his voice disarmed me. I looked up. He held something out in his hand. "What is it?"

"Take it," he said.

It was a rock. A smooth rock, egg-like but not quite. On one small part of its surface it had been engraved with a perfect circle, a white ring. "Is it an Indian symbol?"

"Maybe," he said. "But keep it to yourself. There's only one."

At that moment I wanted more, that's how much I realized what an important gesture it was. I wanted him to say that it was fine that I didn't know how to shoot a gun or that I was afraid of the dark, I wanted him to bend down and touch my shoulder or even tap the side of my leg with his foot. Or maybe it should be me who makes the first move. Maybe I should stretch my arms and ask him to pull me up, and then we could hug and begin all over again, no hard feelings for all the disappointments that came before. Maybe I should dare to say, *Next time you show me how to shoot the rifle.* Yes, maybe that was the way to go.

But before I could get the first word out my father walked away, breaking the small space that opened this level of intimacy between a father and his son.

I didn't call him back because these moments have brief lives, that much I knew. It was like that tiny hummingbird, which might have lived had I let it be. At that moment all that was left to do was to stuff the rock in my pocket and jump to my feet. It was Easter Sunday. The González family packed up its guns and leftovers and put away their found treasures and surprise gifts, leaving no evidence (although no one had seen us arrive) that anything special had transpired in the southern California desert.

Memory Lessons, Memory Lesions

1. On the Pain of Writing Memoir

Like any memoirist who writes so revealingly about family, I'm inevitably asked what my family thinks about my work, which is a diplomatic way of asking how my family feels about my showing the world the intimate portraits of our household. How does my aunt sleep at night knowing one of her nephews has left the curtains opened and that strangers walking by might have caught her standing in the middle of the room while wearing nothing but her old bra? Does my cousin take exception to my writer's graffiti—*My cousin is a drunk!*—on the public stalls? Does my thirty-something younger brother mind being judged for a comment he made when he was only eight years old?

The quick answer is that few members of my family can read what I write. They either don't know how to read, or they don't read English. Both my parents are now dead, so that gives me a certain freedom from guilt or repercussion, and my brother, the only member of my family who holds any interest in my work, loves to read what I write and then shakes his head with disapproval—not at the fact I wrote it down, but at the flaws and follies of the past that we both remember. "Sad," my brother declares each time. "So sad."

Despite these permissions, when I initially set out to write memoir, I did so with plenty of hesitation. First, I had a few excellent models within the Latino literary community to learn from, namely, Esmeralda Santiago, Richard Rodriguez, and Luis Alberto Urrea. I applauded their bravery, their skill at shaping memory into something bigger than themselves, but my own story seemed a little grittier—more sex, more drugs, more rock 'n' roll. And so, I suspected, were theirs. I always thought this was the Latino writer's limitation: the inability to truly and without censorship air out the dirtiest items in the laundry basket. It's a cultural expectation: keep it within the walls of the home, honor the privacy of the living, respect the secrets of the dead.

My earliest attempts at nonfiction certainly adhere to these tenets. I wrote about my elementary school teachers, my first heterosexual crush, the longing for my beloved México after migrating to California. There was a certain childlike innocence that bothered me about what I was writing because even as a child I knew more than I let on, yet here I was, pretending yet again that I didn't. But I wasn't a child anymore. I had lost my innocence a very long time ago. In fact, it had chipped away over the years: after moving to the United States and living in poverty, after enduring years of physical and verbal abuse from my grandfather, after my mother's death, after my father abandoned me, after leaving home as a teenager and never going back, after becoming involved with an abusive lover, after becoming entangled in drugs, alcohol, and the unhealthy lifestyle of many young and careless gay men. Who was I kidding?

I held a very different lens to the world. It was cracked and scratched, and even the prettier things in life appeared somewhat smudged. This didn't necessarily mean that I was walking the earth wrapped inside a cloud of depression—though I had my bad days. It simply meant that when I looked back to the past, when I dug through the rubble of memory, the difficult moments called out to me the loudest. Every hardship longed to be documented as evidence of my perseverance. I had lost so much, and yet I wasn't empty-handed.

I resolved to report my life completely if I was going to speak up at all, especially given another limitation of the Latino family: revisionist memory. When I was younger, I usually questioned my own ability to retain information because I was prone to remembering things a little differently. When I sat down to eavesdrop on the adults talking story, I usually found myself thinking, *That's not how it happened. Did it?* But because I was only a kid, I deferred to the grown-ups and simply adjusted my own version to match theirs. This didn't take place too many times before I realized that what those grown-ups were doing was getting their stories straight. It was an exercise in communal imagination and there were many reasons for changing a story: to protect themselves, their children, or each other; to silence fact; to demonstrate discretion; to recover dignity; to deceive; to deny and to derail previous versions. To deliberately forget was both a good and a bad practice, and these revisions took place in my childhood home repeatedly.

Every family, I suspect, exercises this tactic for keeping the peace, if not ensuring survival. In every class, in every culture, in every corner of the world sits a little house with windows that only shows what its inhabitants want to show. It's a self-imposed code of honor that keeps a semblance of "order," "normativity," and "functionality." (Yes, these *are* ironic quotation marks.) *Nothing alarming happens here,* the window curtains declare when they sway sleepily with the afternoon breeze. Conflict is usually small and containable—a spat over the use of the television, a disagreement about politics, a complaint about a toothpaste cap carelessly dropped into the drain. But the neighbors—now *there's* a family with problems. But not this one, not ours, not here.

I learned the art of delusion early: if a man leaves a bruise, it isn't violence, it's passion; if a woman cries in her sleep it isn't grief, it's her fragile nerves; if a child crumbles inside the anxiety of a toxic household where everyone implodes with rage, sadness, and worry, it isn't family dysfunction, it's his own sensitive nature that's to blame. Give him a cup of chamomile tea and an aspirin. Dab a thimble of alcohol onto his temples and put him to bed. *Nothing's happening, boy. Go to sleep, and tomorrow, when you awake, all will be well again.*

And so my childhood, and so my adolescence, keeping the family sacred while we pitied the neighbors and their unfortunate demonstrations on the front lawn: public fights and other forms of gratuitous theater. We did the same, of course. We yelled and hurled whatever we held in our hands at the moment of outburst; we honked our car horns with hostility; we stomped in and out of the house with resolve. And yet, we were afraid to admit that the neighbors were somehow better than us because they practiced something people in our house seldom did: affection. We saw them kiss hello and good-bye; we marveled at their habit of embracing with spontaneity and joy, even; we saw them touch each other constantly—an arm around the waist, a hand on the shoulder, a flirtatious palm against the buttocks. That was how *they* worked: if they were going to showcase one emotion, they were going to showcase them all. But in the González house we held certain things back. Like displays of love. There was only one way out, and it was finite. There was only one way to look back, and that was by leaving.

Leaving home was the blessing, and even the brute that was Abuelo respected me for that, for accomplishing what no one else had done. For others, there was always the fear of getting lost, of feeling abandoned or without recourse because we were not from this country.

Because I am no longer at home, I am no longer bound to the family codes and no longer under the pressure of my family's immediate scrutiny. And I know that what I write down is simply my version, not the definitive, incontestable truth. Because for something to be true, all one has to do is believe in it, and my family believes wholeheartedly the stories they spin into the family's lore. And so do I. But I am now the creator of the text and therefore in control. That doesn't mean that I am the righteous one, however, or that my remembrance of things past is the most accurate. If anything, I have also learned about my shortcomings, flaws, and mistakes as a history keeper, as a story seeker, and memory excavator. Let me illustrate.

In the summer of 1981 my mother suffered a stroke at the age of thirty, which left her partially paralyzed. One side of her face was frozen in a state of perpetual sadness, and though she was able to express joy with the other side of her face, I never learned to see past the side that seemed to be falling off her skull.

To make matters worse, her ability to speak had been greatly compromised. At the height of her recovery she managed only to slur; when she tired, she was incomprehensible. And always she carried around with her a white handkerchief, which she used to wipe off the spittle that would seep out of the corner of her mouth. Even her laughter was unfamiliar, more like a hiccup than a giggle.

In any case, we learned to move through her illness and slow recovery, through the halls of the blinding white hospitals and the uncertainty of a pending surgery in which a heart valve was to be replaced. The distress paralyzed my mother even further. I knew she was scared. We all were. We had just come into this country a year ago, had just begun to learn this foreign language, and now here we were, making life-changing and life-saving decisions with what little we were told and what little we understood.

Because we were unsure about whether my mother would survive the surgery, we managed a special visitors' visa for my maternal grandparents to come from México to see their ailing daughter before she went into the operating room.

The family reunion was slightly anti-climactic. My grandparents were tired from the long journey up from Michoacán—a three days' trip by bus—and my mother's health had been deteriorating at an alarming speed. I had become a fixture in that hospital room because, at eleven years old, I had picked up more English than anyone else in the family, and I stuttered my way through a communication between my father and the hospital staff. There were a few bilingual nurses floating around but they were in such great demand that we scarcely saw them, so we had to make do with what we had: me.

There we were, my mother, my grandparents, and me, silent and immobile among the unfamiliar contraptions—tubes and lights and metallic boxes—yet another language we did not know in that American hospital. By this time, my mother could no longer speak and I could tell she wanted to say something to my grandparents. They had been holding each other, and kissing and comforting one another with caresses, but that was not enough. My mother had something more to say—a wish, a request, a demand—something. So she resorted to the unthinkable—to writing it down. You see, with only a first-grade education, my mother's writing skills were limited. My grandparents, with no education, couldn't read or write at all. But an effort was made. My mother, fueled by a sense of desperation, wrote a sentence across a piece of paper and showed it to my grandparents.

We were all stunned. My mother knew her parents couldn't read. Since I had been the go-between all this time I thought that maybe I could help and read the sentence for them. But imagine my surprise at the illegible scribble before me. It was neither English nor Spanish. It was a squiggly, loopy design, but it meant something to my mother. She had written something important on that piece of paper.

I knew then that at that moment any one of us could have broken the spell, but through some communal sense of intuition, none of us did. I kept my mouth shut about not being able to read what had been written, and my grandparents considered that scribble thoughtfully, and then nodded their heads. "We understand, Avelina," my grandmother told my mother. "We understand."

Over the years, after moving through the fifth anniversary of my mother's death, then the tenth, the fifteenth, and more recently, the thirtieth, I revisited that moment and thought: What was it that my grandparents had understood? Did they decipher something in that scribble? Was it a symbol and not a string of words that had been drawn on that piece of paper? Or was it something else entirely that they alone had understood? Were they simply humoring my mother, or were they connecting with her in some mysterious way?

I have asked my grandmother three times about it, and each time there has been a different answer. The first time she said that my mother had thanked them for making the long journey north, and that she had asked them to look after my brother and me, should she not survive the surgery. For a long time afterward I believed the first part; the second part, I concluded, was simply my grandmother's wishful thinking.

The next time I asked, my grandmother admitted that there was nothing comprehensible about that script, and that she had simply pretended, hoping that my grandfather had understood, come to find out later that he hadn't either, so they too were left puzzled by the gesture and by the statement scribbled in pencil. They had pondered it very briefly, and then never discussed it again.

But the third time I brought up that incident, my grandmother, perhaps unwilling to revisit that day anymore, simply said she didn't remember. When I became persistent and tried to jog her memory, she grew frustrated and then eventually cried out, "What does it matter anymore? All I have left is the shame that your mother asked us for something and we never understood what it was!"

She burst into tears. And then I burst into tears because as a child I knew when to keep my mouth shut, but as an adult I didn't know any better—because, after all this time, I had finally broken its spell and its memory by overthinking it, overanalyzing it, overscrutinizing it.

For many years after that last exchange with my grandmother, I felt guilty and slightly confused about what I had brought to the surface. My actions had hurt someone I loved. And it made me reflect on my fascination with writing about my family. It made me wonder whether it was wrong, putting my memories into print. I knew it was unlikely that my aunts, uncles, and cousins would ever read them—but their children and grandchildren might. Was it fair, this glimpse into their family's past through someone else's subjective mind? Sadly, I don't have an answer, just the irresistible impulse to write it down.

All these years I have been writing it down. It is how I turn anecdote into meaning and story into significance. It is another way of remembering. And for me, it is also a way to recover what I no longer have—my parents, my childhood, my homeland—to reconstruct the broken days of my past. And in the process of building and rebuilding, I have learned an art. And like any art, memory and memoir is meant to go public, no matter how personal, no matter how painful.

I am no more important than before I wrote it down, though perhaps I am a little wiser through my reliving it. It has become more real—no, it is not the truth, it is experience—human, imperfect, and beautiful. Why then must I justify writing down what I write? Why then am I frequently asked to apologize for the ability to remember? Why then do I get so defensive? I will no longer make excuses because I had no choice to be a witness. I am not a victim of circumstance but rather a participant in one of the many theaters of life. How will I know what role I played if I do not reflect upon it?

Butterfly Boy is my book of memories, and I know that I misremembered a few events, that I have forgotten and suppressed information, that my subconscious might have even made things up to protect myself or others, that—like Akira Kurosawa's *Rashomon*—if other witnesses were called in to give testimony, their stories might not be consistent with mine, but they would be just as valid.

Once upon a time, I even feared that members of my family would read my book and be appalled at how I remember them. But not anymore. That was me, back then. That was them, back then. And I hope they understand that my grown-up eyes see them quite differently now. I also hope they understand that this is what I do—remember—and that this is yet another way for me to love them like I could not before.

2. On What Makes My Memoir Latina/o

The tension between the two words in the phrase "Latina/o memoir" intrigues me. On the left I have a word that homogenizes the disparate populations with roots in the twenty unique countries of Latin America and it offers no knowledge of specific national identities, political struggles, and immigrant trajectories. On the right I have a word that gestures toward individual journey, knowledge, and imagination, a narrative that speaks with the voice of singular observation and perspective.

I suppose then that the union of these two words is as troubling as the conflicts embedded into gender, identity, history, culture, and community—all the key terms that seem to find their way into any literary conversation or book criticism about the works written by Latina/o authors.

But these key terms are also the burdens of any ethnic group, so I can't claim them as particular to the Latina/o experience and thus must think twice before rejecting them as discourse that pigeonholes or stereotypes Latina/o writing.

What then is so Latina/o about the Latina/o memoir?

I am not sure that the answer will be found in a study of either form or content, but through a more abstract ingredient of the creative process: consciousness.

The Latina/o memoir is conscious of movement, particularly vertical movement, particularly from south to north. Whether a writer is first- or second- or third-generation American, somewhere someone moved or migrated or turned around, and more commonly this movement will be connected to some migration in the past or recent past. We are a culture aware of homelands—leaving them, visiting them, imagining them, adopting them, and being nostalgic for the homeland we never knew although our ancestors did. But we are also conscious of social mobility—of bettering ourselves through education and promotion in the labor force—that allows us to find or believe in something else, something newer and improved.

I am reminded of my own family history: how the González clan moved from Zacapu, Michoacán, to the tiny town of Thermal, California, how even in little Thermal we inhabited three distinct residences: in the first we had one bathroom for nineteen people, few beds, and a television on the brink of death; in the second residence we had no bedrooms but we had a car with air conditioning and a television with three working channels; in the third we had our own bedrooms, a refrigerator that didn't need a chair propped against the door to keep it closed, and we had cable.

I can also call this consciousness of movement a consciousness of class. Though we never called ourselves poor or even working class, we were aware of what we didn't have, what we wanted, and what it took to get it—namely, work.

In this way, the Latina/o memoir, like most Latina/o literature, is a working-class narrative—mostly. The truth, however, is that we now have a strong middle-class presence yet it is difficult to find that reality in our books, even though there is also struggle and survival in the professional fields—as many of us in academia can attest. Perhaps I will see more of that middle-class narrative in the next generation of writers but for the most part I haven't seen much of it—although as a community we are conscious of it, and seem to be, through our fierce work ethic, always aiming to get into it or to remain comfortably within it.

The Latina/o memoir is conscious of language and literacy. This is also connected to social mobility, migration, and class consciousness—in the English-speaking United States we have English-speaking households though our names (sometimes) betray a Spanish-speaking birthright or legacy. Each family rejects or preserves the Spanish language in its own way. And each family encourages assimilation or acculturation through either socialized pressures or apathetic stances. No matter if Spanish is preserved or lost or repressed or denied, each family will likely have some symbolic or metaphorical relic or urn or altar that states that Spanish is spoken—or was broken (to invoke Coco Fusco)—there.

Because I am a first-generation English speaker with Spanish as a first language I had no choice but to be bilingual, otherwise I wouldn't have been able to communicate with my grandparents or even my parents. But for me this dual-language existence allowed me to exercise what my family had taught me: movement. I moved from one language to another, each with its own values and sentiments. I had power. I could decipher those official-looking papers that arrived in the mail with angry eagles staring from the small stamp windows in the corner. I could laugh at the jokes and puns told dead-pan by the white-haired comedians on late-night television. But I could also surrender to the nostalgia of my family's stories of the past in places with names like Erongaricuaro and Nahuatzen and Uruapan.

In English I could contradict my mother without her knowing and thus not hurt her feelings. In Spanish I could gripe about my elementary school teachers and their silly homework assignments without offending them. In English I could dream about the future. In Spanish I could reminisce about the past.

The Latina/o memoir then is conscious of split identities and positions, of the tensions between one of this or none of the other or a little bit of both, of the challenges of compromise and capitulation. This is movement again, but it is not geographical, linguistic, or pecuniary, but rather psychological and specifically connected to belonging or not belonging to family, community, and culture. These unstable atoms of emotion are contained within our names and/or our skin colors—those we have or don't have; and they threaten to explode each time we are aware of our differences or when others, against our wishes, set us apart.

Life on the multiple ethnic, cultural, generational, and class identifiers of self has been articulated by our Latina/o theorists in many ways: some (such as Gloria Anzaldúa, Cherríe Moraga, and Alicia Gaspar de Alba) say we straddle a border and/or live on the margin, some (such as Juan Bruce-Novoa and Gustavo Pérez Firmat) say we thrive in the hyphen. Some call it schizophrenic; others define it as a position of dual empowerment. And these places of conflict and reconciliation morph into multidimensional planes when we add other conversations into who we are or who we are not—are we female? are we gay or transgender? are we multiracial or multiethnic?

When I set out to write a gay Chicano memoir I didn't have much in terms of role models—Gloria Anzaldúa and Cherríe Moraga perhaps. Although I did not identify with the feminist act at the time, eventually I became a feminist. Richard Rodriguez was my obvious role model though his pro-assimilationist position didn't quite jibe with my decidedly nationalistic pride: I was proud of my Mexican heritage, and though I eventually identified as a Chicano (the same time I became a feminist—in college), I wanted to connect with a writer who could show me that complex intersection of ethnicity, class, gender, and sexuality.

I didn't find that specific role model but was encouraged to write a Latino memoir anyway because other Latinas/os had done so before me.

By reading books by Latinas/os I also learned that the Latina/o memoir is conscious of politics, of either embracing or rejecting activism—though both are political stances—and whether we like it or not the act of writing and the act of remembering is a political gesture; whether or not we call it political activism, we are performing it. This call to action, this call to the pen, is not about representation—as in representing one's ethnicity, community, or culture, though some will see it that way and either swell with pride or shrink with fear, or something in between. This call to the pen is about responsibility, perhaps even obligation: if you have the privilege of literacy, of voice, of creative power—use it!

When I wrote my coming-of-age, coming-to-America, coming-into-education, and coming-out memoir, I knew that mine was not an individual journey. But until that book was written, my experience felt a bit isolated. I didn't know anyone else who had suffered my silence, that is, until I voiced that suffering and others stepped forward to let me know that they too had suffered or were still suffering, that they too felt alone, once, before they discovered others like them. The fact that mine was not an unusual story did not take away its strength, indeed it only validated the act of breaking silence about such things as domestic abuse in an immigrant household and domestic abuse in a same-sex relationship.

And so the final observation: the Latina/o memoir is conscious of courage. Like many ethnic cultures, Latinos hold a policy against public revelations of trauma and discord and trouble: no one needs to know what's happening inside the walls of the home. Even if the house is collapsing or on fire, no one runs outside and alarms the neighbors. Is it the Catholic in us that teaches us to confess in whispers, hoping that no one else within earshot will hear? Is it our reverence toward our elders, their faults, their imperfections, the fact that we love them anyway that keeps us from disrespecting them by announcing their faults and imperfections to complete strangers?

Some will call it courage, others will call it indiscretion or betrayal, but we do it anyway because the path to healing the damage by telling the story always begins with this first incision: a shaky pen to the paper.

3. On Poetry and the Family Bond

In late October 2006, I was sitting in front of my alma mater's library, where I was tickled to discover that a coffee shop had been set up at the entrance. In ten minutes I was about to participate in a panel for distinguished Arizona State alumni; four of us had been invited back to give an informational, practical chat to students about how to help themselves and their career paths while still in college. My cell phone rang. I knew by the area code that it was one of my relatives from Bakersfield, the California town where I had been born.

"Hello?"

"Mijo?"

"Tía, how are you? Is everything all right?"

"Yes, of course. Did I catch you at a bad time?"

"Well, I have a few minutes before I have to make a presentation. I'm in Arizona."

"Oh, well, a few minutes is all I need. Listen: I wrote a poem."

I flushed. Tía Marta, the woman who married my father's brother, who worked most of her life sorting carrots at a packinghouse alongside my mother and Abuela, who took care of my brother and me, briefly, after our mother died, wrote a poem. Tía Marta, who took lessons in cooking desserts, who had me read and translate recipes on the side panels of cereal boxes, wrote a poem. Tía Marta, barely literate and always laughing, whom I've seen cry only once, when I came to visit her after she left an abusive marriage and who was run out of town by my disgruntled relatives who were furious at her for bringing the González family its first divorce, wrote a poem.

This was a special moment indeed. And it was not the first. After I gave my brother Alex a copy of my first book of poetry, which I had dedicated to him, he was inspired to write a few verses of his own. He wrote two short poems. One was in honor of his recently deceased pet dog, Coqui (a phonetic pronunciation of Cookie—the dog was little). The other was titled "I Wish I Could Cut My Own Hair." He shared with me these two pieces and then, like a true intellectual dummy, I proceeded to analyze them.

"The first poem is about how you're trying to understand death and mortality," I told him. And then I made the terrifying connection between the death of his beloved pet to the death of our beloved mother, and how he was still grappling, like I was, with that loss. How writing this poem was like grieving.

"The other poem is about how you want to be in control," I told him. He stared at me with disbelief, affronted by this act of turning the intimate moment into a lesson, and worse, into an analysis of his state of mind.

"It's just about my dog," he said, flatly. "And about my hair."

"Right," I said, and then I shrank into my seat.

"But you should read *this* poem," he said, pulling out another sheet of paper from a folder. "Our father wrote it."

"Apá wrote a poem?" I said, flabbergasted. My father, with a third-grade education and a unique penmanship that made his letters parade across the page like stick figures, wrote a poem and gave it to my brother to give to me, me, who knew about poetry.

"What is it about?" I asked.

"It's about you and me and our mom," my brother said. "I think he wants to tell the story."

The story. I had been writing my own version, which I called *Butterfly Boy*—an account of the troubled relationship between my father and me after the death of my mother. My father's poem was about meeting a beautiful Mexican lady, marrying her, and raising two sons together. We were not named, exactly. We all appeared in the poem as symbols. My mother was "la estrella"—the star that shone brightly, and then faded, leaving behind two smaller stars to carry her memory into eternity. There was no mention of the fact that "el corazón"—the devastated heart that loved that star—abandoned the two smaller stars to fend for themselves in the fierce open skies. The poem ends on a more hopeful note. *Butterfly Boy* didn't.

"What do you think he's trying to tell us?" my brother asked.

I didn't want to say.

So by the time Tía Marta called to read me her poem over the telephone, I had already learned this: that family members who write poetry are trying to communicate something important. This was different from the poetry written by college students that I had been hearing and reading in workshops over the years that said nothing to me. I also knew that my family simply wanted another poet, their kindred spirit, who understood the role and purpose and impulse of poetry, to listen, to hear what they had to say in the special language of personal expression.

"What is the poem called?" I asked Tía Marta.

The poem was called "Luz"—"Light"—and it is about how life is full of storms and thunder and tempests, how we must each travel through the seas like a lost sailor, looking into the darkness of the clouds, despairingly. But in spite of all that grief, we should be reassured that there is a ray of light worming its way through, biding its time before it strikes its hopeful light upon the soul. She wrote it, she tells me, to give me comfort. Two weeks before, my father had passed away.

"What do you think?" she asked.

"It's beautiful," I replied. "It's the most beautiful poem I've heard in a long time."

We said our quick good-byes. I promised to call her later in the week and I asked her to send me a copy of her poem. She sent it. It became part of my treasury, tucked inside the special folder reserved for my family's art. It has become my two-dimensional paper retablo—secular, yet sacred.

Studies

Andrés Montoya

The Ice Worker Still Sings

1. i believe in the Resurrection

In the year 2000 I received an invitation from the Before Columbus Foundation to celebrate the recipients of the American Book Award. Among the winners listed was *the iceworker sings* by Andrés Montoya, a first book of poetry published by Bilingual Press in 1999, the same year my first book had been released. Although my first book *So Often the Pitcher Goes to Water until It Breaks* had also competed for the American Book Award that year, I considered the volumes companions rather than competitors, and certainly we two Chicano poets had to be compañeros, since both Montoya and I were embarking on a publishing/literary career simultaneously. Seeing the list of winners, however, wasn't the first time I had come across his name or this intriguing title. Just a few years before, Montoya's book had won the Chicano/Latino Literary Prize from the University of California, Irvine, and because I had submitted my manuscript to that competition as well, I subsequently received the announcement of his prize-winning entry.

Indeed I had been overlooked twice in favor of Montoya, but my book had taken a very different path toward acknowledgment and recognition, so I didn't dwell on it. As far as I was concerned, we had both fared well. Besides, my mind was focused on another matter altogether: getting in touch with him.

In the pre–search engine dependence era, I began to seek this fellow poet out via my cohorts. *He's related to the poet José Montoya. He's the son of the painter Malaquías Montoya. He's one of the Fresno poets. He studied with Garrett Hongo and Philip Levine.* The facts of his pedigree thrilled me, and I fantasized about the many pláticas we would have about writing, literature, and the artists we both admired.

I was living in New York City at the time and though I had latched on to the Asian American community of writers—mostly because my then-partner was one of the original founders of the Asian American Writers Workshop—I was feeling particularly disconnected from the politicized Chicano arena of the Southwest. In the Northeast the Latino literary scene was dominated by the Nuyorican spoken word artists and I had been subjected to one too many embarrassing assumptions about both my ethnic identity and my poetics. One notable faux pas occurred when I was invited to a commemorative reading in Spanish Harlem in honor of the recently deceased musical genius Tito Puente. The event was to be televised, and because I was the second reader there was no time to explain to the musician sitting behind me on the stage that my work didn't merit musical accompaniment, which he figured out after the first stanza or so. In the end, he simply clucked his tongue to some rhythm of his own making while I read the title poem of my book. I rushed through the performance, thankful that the cameras didn't capture the sea of confused faces that were sitting before me.

So when the possibility arose of setting up a coast-to-coast pen pal correspondence with the young poet from Fresno and my contemporary (we were less than two years apart in age), I followed through. First, however, I had to make sure I read his work, so that he wouldn't confuse me with some literary tourist who was simply reaching out to him because he had a prize-winning collection of poems or because he had something I didn't have.

I envisioned sending him a copy of my book with my initial letter, signing it: *For a brother in struggle*. I would tell him that I had met his tío José in Davis, California, back in 1993 while he was on the road promoting his book of collected verse, *Information: 20 Years of Joda* and who, when he signed my book—"To Rigoberto from Michoacán"—also thanked me for being the only one in the room who knew to respond *Power*! when he first called out *Chicano*! I would also tell Andrés that I had seen his primo Richard in no less than five performances of Culture Clash, once in New York at a free showing as part of Central Park's Summer Stage Series, and that many of his jokes didn't get a laugh so Richard kept saying, "The one Chicano in the crowd got that one," "The one Chicano in the crowd got that one," and how I wanted to leap up and identify myself as the one Chicano in the crowd, the one who was also feeling a little bit lost and who was madly searching for an umbilical cord back to Aztlán.

Aztlán. The word released a scent into the air, as if I were opening an old box of mementos, testaments to the times of my great awakening. The

Montoyas had been constructing paths toward the politics of Chicano identity and culture for generations, and were important presences in any Chicano Studies curriculum. I remember my former teacher at the University of California, Davis, Francisco X. Alarcón, a legend in Chicano poetry himself, bringing in film, theater, and slides with representations of Chicano art. It was impossible not to swell with pride at the beauty of these unapologetic mirrors that reflected back what many of us had been told to hide, forget, or deny. Among the artists I discovered was Malaquías Montoya—his brush strokes were never silent; they wore the sound of pain and sweat and strength.

That semester, in the spring of 1993, Maestro Alarcón walked into the classroom in tears because both César Chávez and Cantinflas had just died, one right after the other. Their legacies became more urgent than ever and we rushed into stories: those of us who came from farmworking families admitted to it; those of us who had been tickled by the Mexican comic recalled his antics and remembered watching his black-and-white movies in the living rooms of our youth while sitting with our parents or grandparents. And then Maestro Alarcón took us to the fancy de Young museum in San Francisco to absorb an exhibition of pre-Columbian artifacts; and then Maestro Alarcón put us on the local radio to read our poems and we read them nervously and with slight embarrassment that we had gotten all gussied up only to be heard and not seen; and then Maestro Alarcón took us to a party at La Galería de la Raza in Sacramento, where an older generation of writers were telling stories about the days of the Brown Berets in the 1970s, and I remember how touching it was that they kept declaring that it was us, the next generation in the 1990s, who would keep the revolutionary spirit circulating on this earth once they were gone. And that is how a Chicano shapes a Chicano. How could I not be part of a larger mission after that? How could I not seek out my allies?

So, Andrés, fellow poet, fellow Chicano, will you be that ally? Will you keep me grounded to the world of the Central Valley farmlands where my family picked grapes? Will you look for me in the city of the skyscraper and the subway and the twenty-four-hour bodegas where I can find any word from any part of the world, except for the word "Chicano"? Andrés Montoya, will you please write back?

Oddly enough, in the few exchanges I had about Montoya with other writers, no one mentioned the most vital piece of information: that he was deceased. It wasn't until I received his book in the mail, sat back on the couch, and prepared myself for a pleasant trip back to Califas, that my heart stopped when reading the opening phrase of his bio: *The late Andrés Montoya . . .*

A great sense of loss consumed me. The pangs became greater still as I read stunning poem after stunning poem. Manhattan was getting larger and lonelier by the minute as the streets outside the apartment grew louder with the rush-hour traffic. But by the end of the first read-through, when the evening had settled into the tranquility of dusk and dinnertime, I understood why no one had mentioned that Andrés Montoya had died. Andrés Montoya's voice was not silent; it was very much alive.

2. coming forth from this earth, this dirt

I will argue that in the Chicano literary sphere there are two city names that get invoked more than any other: El Paso and Fresno. Those in the know, those who read and appreciate Chicana/o letters, will probably conclude that it's not much of an argument. It's fact. I have ceased to be surprised when I hear that another poet situates his/her work if not his/her familial history in either of these places. The lineage is extensive and impressive. I once joked to a friend, there must be something in the water, or, as Estela Portillo Trambley once declared, the air. Blame all those pollutants of ASARCO in Texas. And in the case of the Central California Valley, blame the pesticides.

Though I can write at length about the phenomenon that is the El Chuco "Xicanorati"—to borrow the term from Lorna Dee Cervantes—I want to focus on Fresno, and poetry in particular. About El Chuco I will simply say that I have come to know the one hundred (and counting) versions and visions of the city and its surroundings so intimately over the years from the novels of John Rechy, Arturo Islas, Benjamin Alire Sáenz, and Alicia Gaspar de Alba, to the stories of Estela Portillo Trambley, Richard Yañez, Christine Granados, and Sergio Troncoso, to the poetry of Ricardo Sánchez, Pat Mora, and Sheryl Luna. And, of course, the writings of Dagoberto Gilb, Ray Gonzalez, and José Antonio Burciaga. The list goes on. I was not surprised to end up a book reviewer for *The El Paso Times* because the activist fervor, complex and conflicted that it sometimes can be, continues to run through every vein of the community—and quite palpably through the arts. El Paso is, after all, a linguistic, cultural, sociopolitical border mecca of clashing and colliding perspectives. I have been there countless times via the written word, and it's a place I look forward to revisiting.

Likewise I have come to know the Fresno of the poetic imagination. Although readers and critics make reference to "the Fresno school" of poetry, a class-conscious sensibility that includes Gary Soto and Juan Felipe Herrera, as well as the poets Philip Levine and Larry Levis, the common ground usually ends there because, aesthetically, these poets travel very disparate terrains. But that speaks to the city's awesome ability to embrace and nurture the many creative paths out and back into its cultural corazón. In the next generation, the list of Central Valley poets who have published notable books includes Blas Manuel de Luna, David Dominguez, and of course, Andrés Montoya. (Very male dominant, I realize, but Chicana/o literature also has the unique distinction of having a very female-dominant list of fiction writers.)

So, what is so remarkable about Fresno, the crown jewel of the San Joaquin Valley, the sixth largest city in California? Like many California towns, Fresno has grown to become a sizable urban center, swallowing up land and water resources that were once the domain of the agricultural business. Each year there is less demand for employment in harvesting grape, tomato, almond, and nectarine (among 250 other crops) and more in the food processing plants such as the plant that packages the Sun Maid raisins thereby christening Fresno the Raisin Capital of the World. And there are other businesses that have moved in, taking advantage of the cheap land. Like Gap, for example, whose distribution site squats over no less than eighty fertile acres of soil.

The population has grown steadily, though it continues to be mostly white, followed closely by, according to the census bureau, "Latinos of all races." At last count the general population was well over a million for the entire metropolitan area; its increase fed by the Los Angeles residents relocating from the south and the San Francisco residents relocating from the north, many of them tempted there by affordable middle-class housing. Indeed the city has been working tirelessly for decades to manufacture a certain image of itself by building large cultural and commercial attractions: a fancy museum, where fans of American literature can browse through the William Saroyan Gallery (Saroyan, you know, was a Fresno native), and a fancy coliseum, where lucky ticket holders can attend concerts given by music industry icons such as The Rolling Stones.

But the aforementioned statistics, demographics, and revitalization efforts are matters of public record, which awakens my curiosity: Where, then, can I find the more private matters? That is, those neighborhoods not included on the city's street-sweeper route? Those brown spaces, those Chicano spaces, that house the laborers—from the farmworkers to the driver of the street-sweeping truck—and those spaces where the great ash tree casts a different light, and so too a different kind of shadow? The city spaces witnessed by Montoya in his poem "fresno, august '92," which reads:

> the brown boy lies dead   spit slipping red
> from his mouth   in bubbles   to the dry cracked dust
> of the ground   sucking it up   like the juice
> of a stepped-on orange.

To find my way to the barrio streets, those left out of the annals of Fresno history, those unmentioned by the tourist pamphlets, though not forgotten in its demonizing newspaper headlines, I listen for the songs of the ice worker.

Indeed, the ice worker sings very sad songs. And in the embattled but spiritual world of Montoya's poetry, he comes across as a messenger, a Gabriel trumpeting the burdens of the working class. But he's more like a soul in purgatory whose mission is "to sing of the imminent return of justice." In fact it's what makes him more human than angel, more tragic than vainglorious: "no roses will fall from my eyes to bury you."

To misconstrue the elegant elegy of Montoya's tone as pessimism is to misunderstand the ice worker's poetics:

> . . . mostly, he would steal the beats
> and put in his own words about life,
> about love, about dying.
> this is how he became a poet
> parting ways with the sad ocean
> of ordinary speech.

It's called survival, muscle-twitching strength limned with hope, this act of inhabiting, not romanticizing, struggle and then articulating that existence with lyrics "to alleys and trash cans, / to ants and the crushed peach of their affection." It's not called complaint. Discontent means someone else—someone from the outside—has the power to change, appease, or even fix the problems plaguing the displeased. But outrage means that the burden of change is everybody's: insider, outsider, brown, white.

Violence is highlighted in Montoya's work. And though his poems tell the heartbreaking stories of Jesse and René, victims of the "corrupt hands" of cops who walk about "with their .357 smiles," and though the ice worker bemoans the loss of youth, the immediate targets of the street wars ("a maya warrior dies in the streets of fresno / never realizing who he was"), he also holds the Chicano community accountable and subsequently calls upon the residents to search within, to strive for reflection and consciousness, the first step toward action:

and where raza are our heroes
the heroes of aztlán?

what became of that great nation we were going to build?
where did all the warriors go with their sharpened knives
and loaded rifles?

This "call to arms" is metaphorical, of course, not literal. Montoya is not endorsing a coup d'état, though he's certainly demanding us to "fight back." If the passion of the language unsettles us, then the work is accomplishing its task. Montoya's poems are not the static crime scene photographs or the quaint glimpses through the windows of the barrio—they are the shattering of glass, the gun shots, the shouting or the wailing that pierces through walls:

can you hear it now
life in the middle of it all
this field of dust and poison
and pain like a perfectly orchestrated song
whelping out its measure of silence?

Another important theme in Montoya's poems is his engagement of Christianity. There's as much Jesus in this book as there is in a Catholic church, but this Jesus, "a Murdered Man, the murdered king," is at times the sacrosanct provider of faith, and at other times he's a humanized martyr susceptible to the derision of those who have lost their faith:

Christ came walking up blackstone avenue
and i dragged him into an alley
and spit in his face. he didn't say anything
  and it pissed me off.

Or, even more dramatically, a victim of those who confuse a downtrodden Jesus for other disenfranchised peoples:

> this is the silence of Christ beaten blue
> and black on the scorching streets
> of the city, Christ mistaken for a gangster
> or thug or just another mojado moving
> in on the precious property of "providence."

And just when it appears that the ice worker has reached the breaking point ("i'm just a chicano, an indian / who sees life swallowed up in a dream and wants to implode") and about to succumb to despair ("something tearless / bellows from my belly"), part IV comes along, slightly different in tone, with its dozen or so mentions of the word "love" or "lover," as if, all along, we have been ignoring that these poems are as much an homage to a city as they are an indictment. Reread the final poem in the book, "fresno night," and understand this, all of you, Fresno, its citizens, and readers whose eyes have come to see "the cold metal madness of this city": not all who enter here have abandoned hope.

This is Montoya's Fresno, a place in need of a spiritual cleansing by way of a Chicano revolution. But so too is it a place that deserves it. As do other places we inhabit that we both revile and adore. *the iceworker sings* shines a light on the city in a troubled time, but this tension became the muse that pressured and prodded its poet to that dangerous space, what Federico García Lorca calls *duende,* where artists risk everything to understand—and survive—their damaged world.

3. landscapes of sadness

Montoya, like Gary Soto, acknowledged the deceased poet Ernesto Trejo by including in his collection a poem to him in memoriam. In turn, Blas Manuel de Luna included, in his book *Bent to the Earth* (2005), a poem in memory of Andrés Montoya, and Manuel Paul López set Part 15 of his long poem "Go, Nijinsky, Go," in his book *Death of a Mexican* (2006) as a letter addressed to Montoya. I'm making a mental note of those Chicano writers who have passed recently, who have also been remembered, honored, and celebrated by the many communities to which they belonged: Víctor Martínez, Angela de Hoyos, Alfred Arteaga, Omar Salinas, raulrsalinas, Gloria Anzaldúa, Lalo Delgado, Roxana Rivera. I don't dare go farther back, because this list—indeed this loss—is daunting. But grief is part of the human condition. Every culture acknowledges it and employs ceremonies and symbols that allow entire groups of people to participate in a shared experience of grief. No one bears the burden alone, though certainly each person must come to terms with it individually.

I've always been touched by descansos, those makeshift memorials on the sides of roads or streets, usually consisting of a cross, flowers, and a votive candle, that give passersby notice to give respect: *Somebody died here*. I have come across many of these descansos marking accident sites on the highways of México or in the Southwest. But so too have I seen them in Manhattan—in the center of Chelsea, no less, where a scaffold collapsed, killing a Mexican day laborer. In the Chicano neighborhoods these descansos take other shapes: the mural, the silkscreen T-shirt, the tattoo. And then, there is the descanso-poem.

The first time I came across the descanso-poem was in Thermal, California, where my family arrived from Michoacán in 1980. There were two distinct groups accessible to the youth: the farmworkers and the cholos. There was a very thin distinction between these groups because all of our fathers worked in the fields and our mothers in the packinghouses. And it took very little time for the farmworker boys, once they hit puberty, to adopt the chino pants and the hairnet. But there were some, like the recent immigrants already in adolescence or on the cusp of adolescence (i.e., my cousins and I), who didn't adopt that identity mainly because we didn't speak their language—English. And of all of us, it was me who picked it up, not only because I didn't resist, but because I wasn't resentful that I had been plucked from my familiar neighborhood to come here, to this sleepy little unexciting town that would not make national headlines until someone reproduced the Elvis stamp on the exposed side of the post office many years later. And though there was always talk among the adults about going up north to Bakersfield, where I had been born, where the family toiled before we went back to México, we stayed put in the Coachella Valley.

A year later I could hold my own, navigating English like a native, though this was only useful in school or whenever some document came in the mail. Otherwise, Spanish was everywhere—at home, at the market, at the post office, at work. But the streets, which in the evenings were the domain of the young adults, were in English.

Being the shy kid that I was, I preferred to stay at home after sunset. The grown-ups warned us about the dangers "out there," with *those* cholos and *their* drugs and *their* violence. As evidence of that, they pointed out how the police were always patrolling the trailer park where many of those cholos lived. We kids simply believed their words, which were proven right when we heard of a knife fight that left a young man dead.

The next day the school was a-buzz over the incident and many claimed to have witnessed the confrontation, providing exaggerated details as proof of it. And when word spread that there would be a vigil that night, my cousins and I seized on it, looking forward to participating in something exciting for a change.

Somehow three of us, the oldest males, made it out of the apartment that evening. Because Thermal was a small place, and we all knew where that trailer park was located, off we went, no doubt hoping to have our own tales to tell the next day at school. But what we came across surprised me. The gathering was somber and dignified, just like the funerals back in México, with nothing extraordinarily different or out of place. When some of the young men spoke, their voices were low, so the crowd had to remain hushed in order for all to hear. The speakers talked about El Tony, but they talked about themselves as well, as if this was the gift of El Tony's passing: the chance for anyone to participate and give themselves context, and to exercise the expression of voice in the language or sentiment shared with the person who no longer speaks.

My cousins were anxious to leave because it was clear that nothing explosive was going to happen, and just as we were about to step out of the gathering, a piece of paper was handed to me by a young woman in heavy makeup and teased hair—a chola with penciled-in eyebrows. I looked at this piece of paper, a poem dedicated to El Tony, all of it written in calligraphy and centered on the page. Everyone clutched their keepsake respectfully, and so did I, taking it home with me and poring over it all night trying to decipher what the poem meant, what it told me about El Tony, and about the poet who had been moved to inspiration. How intimate this gesture, sitting down to remember, to envelop memory with metaphor, to give it texture by committing it to print, and then letting it go, watching it circulate as it relayed its solemn message to other readers: *Somebody died here*. But the affection for that somebody continues.

For Chicano writers, the act of memorializing is essential. We have been doing this even before we started calling ourselves Chicanos. From the protest rallies to los encuentros at community centers, from El Teatro Campesino to Con Tinta, from the loose-leaf descanso-poems, we remember, we don't forget, we write it down for ourselves and others. Memory means presence of history. History means we have a past, and most definitely a viable future. And the act of recognizing a fellow writer, one of our own, means we are a movement that has benefited from the contributions of those now gone, and that will continue its volition as long as those still living exercise the agency of language and voice.

I learned from those young people at the trailer park, if we don't remember each other, if we don't speak for ourselves in our own tongues, no one else will, because, cholos or Chicano writers, we are still relatively invisible, ignored, and, yes, deemed insignificant by the dominant groups. We risk erasure at every turn, even from our own communities, where we are also not read or understood. I know these statements sound dramatic, but how many times do our works appear on the shelves of mainstream booksellers, or in college curricula outside of Chicano Studies courses, or on the shortlists of book award nominations. Think about how the extent of knowledge from our young people usually doesn't extend beyond Sandra Cisneros's *The House on Mango Street.* When I expressed these concerns before, my friend Richard Yañez reminded me, "We have been here before all of those things and we will be here afterward." And he's right, but to secure that continuum, memory must be planted, nurtured, harvested.

Writers leave their legacy in print. Writers reach out, even after their deaths. Those epistolary poems of Montoya's, letters addressed to KB, Sarah, and Antonio, among others, are also letters to the general reader. Yes, they are his letters to the world that never wrote to him, to invoke Emily Dickinson.

Andrés Montoya is not dead; he is very much alive.

I never knew Montoya personally; I never had the chance. But I know his work, and I respect and admire it immensely. And having read (and reviewed) so many worthy books of poetry written by Chicanas/os and Latinas/os, I make the following declaration very much informed by what has been written and published in the past: In this generation, *the iceworker sings* should be acknowledged as the finest book of poetry to come out of our community. It should receive even greater acclaim, but alas, as I have stated before, so much of what we write remains relatively unheard, unread, marginalized, regionalized, and shrouded in silence. It is our responsibility that these works, and Montoya's especially, travel outside of our borders and that they do not stay silent.

One effort to honor his memory has been in place since 2004, the year the inaugural winner of the Andrés Montoya Prize for a book of poems by an emerging Latina/o writer was published. The Chicana poet Sheryl Luna received the honor for her book *Pity the Drowned Horses.* Since then, the winners have included the Chicano poets Gabriel Gómez for *The Outer Bands* (2006) and Paul Martínez Pompa for *My Kill Adore Him* (2008), the Cuban American poet Emma Trelles for *Tropicalia* (2010), and more recently Laurie Ann Guerrero, another Chicana from Texas like Luna, for her book *A Tongue in the Mouth of the Dying* (2012). The contest is held every two years and is supervised by Nicaraguan American poet Francisco Aragón, the program director of Letras Latinas, a literary program of the Institute for Latino Studies at the University of Notre Dame.

There is also a rumor that Bilingual Press will soon publish a posthumous book of poems by Montoya, tentatively titled *colón-ization,* edited by Montoya's friend, the Chicano writer Daniel Chacón. Over a decade has passed since the publication of *the iceworker sings.* It's about time for that second book to appear in print.

I'd like to close this essay with Montoya's own words, with a few of the many lines that have inspired many readers, including me, to keep up the good fight, to express anger, but also beauty, to celebrate the world we live in, and to imagine the world we want, to avoid complacency, and, above all to remember, to perform activism with ink:

> i will cry for resistance and struggle, for your song
> like the song of our murdered ancestors
> joining in the marrow of bones
> fire running though veins.

The Poet Ai

An Appreciation

When the poet Ai passed away on March 20, 2010, very few details surfaced about the circumstances of her death. Even the report of her passing moved very slowly through the social networking channels. I found out through a text from a friend who came across an unconfirmed statement made by a virtual friend on Facebook. And then silence, not so much as a follow-up from anywhere. I e-mailed, made phone calls, sent more texts, searched Twitter, Google, and the Blogosphere, and I either came across others who were searching for any snippet of information like I was, or upon entries that began, "I never read this poet before but . . ." Or even more devastatingly, "I never heard of her but . . ."

Because it was the weekend I knew the University of Oklahoma (where she held a professorship) would not be posting any official statement until Monday at the earliest, I spent two days feeling pained and frustrated about the lackluster response from the poetry community at large, especially from the younger poets who were always quick to grieve for other writers, no matter what level of the dead writer's acclaim or accomplishment. Just the previous month, we had lost Lucille Clifton, and everybody, it seemed, had some connection to the poet and/or her poems. The online tributes and cyber-celebrations collided with each other because there were so many expressions of sadness and appreciation for one of America's most beloved poets.

That's when it hit me. The stark contrast between Ai and Lucille Clifton, two women of color, roughly ten years apart in age and who were both practitioners of the dramatic monologue, were glaringly obvious: Clifton was a public and visible figure, anyone in the field could stake a claim to a relationship with her; Ai was private, with such a small online presence that even locating her poems on the Internet produces negligible results. Clifton's poetry, at times autobiographical, even in their darkest moments shone with light; Ai's persona poems, even when they gestured toward the light, were terrifying. Encounters with the amiable Lucille Clifton (aka Mama Lucille), age seventy-three and a grandmother at the time of her death, were usually characterized as generous, she was a woman who had grown comfortable in her maternal and nurturing image. Stories about Ai, who was sixty-two, lean and elegant, single and childless, were, well, complicated. I will dispense with regurgitating other people's experiences, those are theirs to keep or give away. I will speak instead about the Ai that I pieced together, and how it was appropriate that she leave this world with as much of the mystery and intensity that she put into it through her poetry. This is my tribute to Ai.

The first time I saw Ai was around 1996, when we both lived in the college town of Tempe, Arizona. I was completing an MFA degree at Arizona State, and Ai, who taught occasionally for the writing program (though never during my tenure there), maintained her residence there because of the area's low rent. Money matters would become a common theme whenever I heard anything in Tempe about Ai, but they were spoken less out of malice and more as a cautionary tale about the struggles of living the life of a poet. Ai had garnered some of the nation's top literary prizes—the Guggenheim, the NEA grant (twice!), a fellowship from the Radcliffe Foundation, the Lamont Poetry Prize from the Academy of American Poets—and here she was, trying desperately to make ends meet. All of these rumors came together when I sat in the back row to listen to Ai read at Changing Hands Bookstore on Mill Avenue.

I will not lie: Ai was a terrible reader of her work. She rushed through the lines and spoke too softly, her face rarely changing expression as she delivered each piece with the same flat tone. I caught maybe every other phrase, and would have sneaked out of the room if I could, but because I was trapped there in that cramped little space, I focused instead on Ai herself—her hair pulled back dramatically, her long neck, graceful and attractive. I couldn't exactly pinpoint her ethnicity: she looked black, but with Asian features, and she wore an elaborate display of Native American jewelry. She had changed her name, I had been told, to this Japanese word. It meant "love." And though Ai was a homonym for "I" as in "me," there was very little of her in the poetry. Her poems were not about Ai, they were about others. The poem she had just read was a piece about O. J. Simpson. "I had to dispense with the dedication," she explained, "because my publisher thought we might get sued."

Despite that disappointing initial encounter, I still went to the college library to find her work, encouraged by my peers who assured me that she was much better on the page than on the stage. And that's how I came across *Cruelty* on the dusty shelves, and that's how I will remember *really* being introduced to the poet Ai.

First published in 1973 by Houghton Mifflin, the forty-four poems in *Cruelty* are also the shortest poems she ever published. Eventually she would favor the extended narrative pieces, lengthy dramatic monologues that invoked historical and popular figures, but the poems in her first book were tight as fists and punched the reader in the face with their one-, two-, or three-stanza blows.

Though the book is not divided into sections, there is a pattern to the parade of voices: the poems usually alternate from male speaker to female speaker, no gender dominates though there is a clear gender struggle in the relationships those voices speak of. All but two of the poems are first person. The two exceptions are "Hangman" (written in the third person) and "Warrior" (written in the second person) and are oddities in other ways: "Hangman," about a traveling executioner setting up his scaffold, securing the trap door, and testing the rope, has a particular medieval feel to it, except that the poem also mentions silos and Kansas, creating an anachronism that's difficult to reconcile among the other realist and more contemporary-sounding pieces. "Warrior" describes a Native American male preparing for battle in what's arguably a precolonial setting because the war is waged against "rival villages" and the white man appears to be completely absent from his consciousness.

The only other poems that reach far back into history are the poems "1931" and "New Crops for a Free Man," with its phrase "free man" situating it during the slavery era. The more intriguing of these two is "1931." Set during the Great Depression, the poem very quietly weaves the country's economic woes into one man's loveless union: he says to his significant other just after he picks up his infant son, "Before you only gave yourself out of boredom / and with this hunger, even that is gone."

It's interesting to note that "1931" also hints at the speaker's racial identity. When he looks at his son, "His irises, two blue, baby onions / come apart as he wakes." A blue-eyed baby, most likely a white baby, and white parents. Very few of Ai's poems in *Cruelty* contain markers of ethnicity or race. The most notable examples, however, are "New Crops for a Free Man" and "Woman to Man" in which the speaker is a black woman who revels in the aggressive sexual power she has over a white man:

We don't mix, even in bed,
where we keep ending up.
There's no need to hide it:
you're snow, I'm coal,
I've got the scars to prove it.
But open your mouth,
I'll give you a taste of black
you won't forget.

Other rather obvious examples are the poems "The Sweet" with its "Eskimo prostitute" and "Cuba, 1962," in which a Cuban sugarcane farmer lops off the feet of his dead lover, Juanita, and declares: "Whoever tastes my woman in his candy, his cake, / tastes something sweeter than this sugar cane; / it is grief." This is also the only poem in the book that mentions a person by their given name.

Aside from these anomalies, the majority of the poems in *Cruelty* do not embrace a particular race, historical timeline, or geography (though some critics argue it's mainly set in the American Southwest), but it does suggest (and maintains) a preoccupation with the working class. And more specifically, with the sexual tensions and desires of rural people. There are very few material possessions mentioned in *Cruelty*, and they are usually hand-held objects such as an axe, a shotgun, boots, an assortment of kitchen utensils, in addition to cars and trucks. And though the landscape may trap or limit these figures within a social economic setting, the traumas and dramas of their very ordinary lives make of them larger-than-life human beings.

Indeed *Cruelty*'s opening poem "Twenty-Year Marriage" starts out with explosive sexual energy in which the female speaker's appetite for her husband grows by the second as she waits in the truck "with its one good wheel stuck in the ditch" while the man takes his time urinating at a nearby tree. Perhaps it's the sight of his exposed organ that sets her imagination going, but her excitement escalates to the point of wanting to be completely penetrated by him, wanting to be entered the way he would enter the truck:

I'm the same size, shape, and make of twenty years ago,
but get inside me, start the engine;
you'll have the strength, the will to move.
I'll pull, you push, we'll tear each other in half.

The woman celebrating the pleasures of the flesh places this poem in the realm of feminist expression, though today's feminists might take issue with the way the speaker objectifies herself as an old truck. Nothing is easily reconciled in Ai's poetry. In the poem "Old Woman, Young Man" the female speaker makes the empowering statement, "Unashamed, I part my legs," to which her young lover responds, *"look there's a rose, / yes, but it's lost its teeth."* Equally empowering is the poem "Woman to Man," in which the black woman assumes the role of stealthy predator ("I won't see how afraid / to be with me you are") highlighting the race war taking place because of the lover's whiteness.

Without this agency and the female's sexual satisfaction, there is cruelty, hence the title poem in which the female speaker bemoans her lover's impotence ("Can't you see? / The thing I want most is hard, / running toward my own teeth / and it bites back."). Or the poem "The Rivals" in which the speaker, twenty years younger than her lover, resorts to the use of a sausage as a sexual aid.

Looking back at that opening poem, it is a deceptive beginning to the book because there is very little happiness in the relationships that follow. The narrative of the unhappy couple comes in many forms: the alienated lovers in "The Estranged" ("I strain at keeping you with me"); the unfaithful wife in "Possessions" ("I wait for you to ask me how it was with the other man"); the on-again/off-again relationship in "Why Can't I Leave You?" ("I pick up my suitcase and set it down, / as I try to leave you again"); and the man who chooses the company of a sow to his wife—as he lies down next to the animal in the sty, he hears his wife calling him and, referring to himself in the third person, he frets, "How can I tell her he will never come?"

If the politics and conflicts of sex are manifested as troubled relationships, then one of the adverse effects, violence, stands close by. This rage or anger can take many forms, and is as individual a practice as the person committing the act; but in *Cruelty* the rage and anger can be generally characterized as domestic, cruel acts that take place within the walls of the home (usually psychological and physical abuse), or senseless random acts on the street (in the wrong place at the wrong time).

Though the landmark case *Roe v. Wade* rooted itself into American popular culture and society in 1973, the same year *Cruelty* was published, Ai was already exploring the complexities of terminating a pregnancy. In the second poem in the book, a ten-line piece called simply "Abortion," a man walks in to find his lover lying in bed, her stomach "flat as an iron" and the male fetus "wrapped in wax paper." It's important to note that this was the woman's choice—she warned her lover she'd do it. What's not clear is whether this was an act of revenge, an act of desperation, or a necessity based on economic hardship. The end result, however, is that the woman takes control of the situation and the lover affirms his loyalty: "Woman, loving you no matter what you do, / what can I say, except I've heard / the poor have no children, just small people / and there is room only for one man in this house."

It's interesting that children, childbirth, and pregnancies are presented as causes for distress and loss in the world of *Cruelty*: an abortion as power play; a death at childbirth as an act of mercy; a pregnancy as a prelude to miscarriage or a painful birth. In the poems set in the rural landscape, these anxieties are shaped by an environment without the privileges of prenatal care or other medical attention. But not every horrible action can be explained or contextualized so neatly. Take, for example, the abusive mother in the poem "Child Beater," one of Ai's more well-known and terrifying pieces. After forcing her seven-year-old, undernourished child to crawl on the floor to reach her dinner bowl, all the while beating her with a belt, she goes to the closet to grab a chain leash. Once the child reaches the bowl, she whirls the leash around her head as she says: "O daughter, so far you've only had a taste of the icing, / are you ready now for some cake?"

Two other examples of physical violence (this time between lovers) includes "Prostitute," in which the woman shoots her husband (most likely also her pimp) and then walks out wearing his boots and carrying his gun; and "Recapture," in which a woman runs off, only to be caught by her abusive lover who, after he beats her, demands that she perform fellatio: "Come on, bitch of my love," he says, "while it is still easy."

These illustrations of cruelty will not appeal to many readers or may seem shocking, even in today's society in which violence and pornography is easily accessible through television and video games. It would be easy to declare that the times have caught up to the poet Ai, but in reality the world has always been full of violence and heartbreak and Ai's work does not allow us to romanticize, sanitize, or dehistoricize the past. Her poems are testaments that prove untrue the characterization of America's history as innocent, as simpler times with better days. Ai writes about the tough times, the troubled lives, and the leaner days that most would rather forget or erase.

There is little glory, however, in remembering; only completeness of story. And if the heroes and martyrs have staying power in the history books, then here to encroach on that sacred space are the psychopaths and the mad misogynists: enter the vagrant in "The Hitchhiker," who stabs the good Samaritan in the chest with his switchblade and then takes off with her car, feeling not a shred of guilt as he rides off into the sunset; enter the young soldier in "The Deserter" who, without provocation, shoots the old woman who put him up and then takes off with her meager supply of vegetables; and finally enter the fury of the jumper in "The Suicide" who says:

> The wharf has a tight, deep vagina of water
> and I'm going to fuck it until it novas,
> just to let everybody see
> how I cut through life like a diamond
> in a sack of glass, with no regrets
> and what's it to you
> to shove up your ass.

The flesh, its pleasures and pains, its seductions and repulsions, its comforts and damages, its promiscuity and wrath, gives these nameless, anonymous people breath—they love and hurt, and therefore they exist, they are real. It's important not to lose sight of the fact that these are also working-class folk whose everyday urgencies are not only about survival but about psychological interiority, which is why the two complex spaces most often mentioned in the book are the bedroom and the kitchen: there's sleeping and eating, yes, but also fucking and fighting. To call them tragic figures, to call them noble, is to slip into pity or condescension, it is not to understand that they are visible on their own terms, even outside of our line of sight.

The next time I stumbled into Ai was in the Changing Hands Bookstore again, a symbolic return to the source. We were both browsing the used bookshelves, she unsuspecting that I was, in fact, stalking her from a distance, enthralled and dazzled by the author of a book that had validated my own poetics of violence in my yet-unpublished book, *So Often the Pitcher Goes to Water until It Breaks*. I revisited the manuscript and made two drastic changes: I got rid of the sections, allowing the poems to flow uninterrupted from beginning to end, like Ai's first book. I then moved the poem "The Slaughterhouse" to the beginning in order to open the book with a *Cruelty* bang.

I like to think that these choices are part of what attracted Ai to select my book as one of the winners of the National Poetry Series in 1998. I had moved to Albuquerque by then, and had enrolled in a PhD program, which I dropped by the end of the first year, convinced that I was a writer, not a scholar. And because I no longer had a compelling reason to stay in New Mexico, I decided to move and take my chances in a bigger city: New York.

The call that summer from the National Poetry Series administrators gave me that push, though when they revealed to me that it was the poet Ai who had selected my book I quickly clarified that I didn't know her personally, even though we had lived in the same Arizona town. "We know," the voice on the phone said. "Ai already told us." I didn't think to ask for Ai's phone number or mailing address, so I decided to thank her my own way: by absorbing Ai's second book, *Killing Floor.*

Published in 1979, also by Houghton Mifflin, six years after *Cruelty, Killing Floor* contains only twenty-four poems, all but six of the speakers are male, and it bears the following dedication: *to the ghosts.* If sex and violence are the belly and the groin of *Cruelty,* then death is the spleen of *Killing Floor.*

This second book is a bridge between Ai's celebrated debut with its powerful snapshots of commonplace people and the dramatic monologues she would continue writing for the rest of her literary career—persona poems inspired by figures of history, politics, and pop culture.

The title poem imagines Trotsky's fears and anxieties from his days as a Bolshevik revolutionary in Russia to his exile in México, where he is eventually assassinated; the hands that wielded the pickaxe, "a black dove on whose back I ride." Two celebrated Japanese writers, Yukio Mishima and Yasunari Kawabata, make brief but startling appearances in the poems that imagine the moments before their deaths. Ai delves into Mishima's most intimate layers as she constructs and weaves in "Nothing But Color" the details of his homosexual desire and his ritual suicide by suppuku in 1970. The ascent into the spirit world can be seen as a type of coming out:

> I start pulling my guts out,
> those red silk cords,
> spiraling skyward,
> and I'm climbing them
> past the moon and the sun,
> past darkness
> into light.

In "Talking to a Reflection in a Shallow Pond," Kawabata's consciousness splits in two and the abuse one inflicts on the other gestures toward the Nobel laureate's depression and eventual suicide, just a few years after the suicide of his friend, Yukio Mishima.

Two other tragic and well-known figures worth mentioning are Marilyn Monroe in the poem "She Didn't Even Wave," which places Marilyn in her earlier manifestation, Norma Jean Baker, attending her birth mother's funeral; and "I Can't Get Started," which tracks the final hours of Ira Hayes, the Native American war veteran who was one of the six figures memorialized in the iconic photograph of the flag-raising at Iwo Jima. Hayes died at the age of thirty-two, frozen to death of exposure after a night of heavy drinking, hence the final lines of the poem, "I'm the one dirty habit / I just can't break."

The conceit of taking a person whose fame, notoriety, or infamy is common knowledge and then dramatizing a scene from their private lives is a challenging onus that requires skill: there's the burden of facts and the demand on the reader to expand his/her definition of a personality whose identity is constricted by a popular image. When Ai handles notable literary and historical figures, such as Trotsky, Mishima, Kawabata, and Hayes, persons whose intellectual and heroic acts seem to be removed from the details of their personal lives, there's plenty of room to give these figures additional dimensionality through the persona poem, especially when there's some element of their being that has remained relatively unexplored, such as Trotsky's paranoia, Mishima's homosexuality, Kawabata's depression, and Hayes's PTSD.

But when dealing with figures such as Marilyn Monroe, whose intimate life has been excavated to the point of evisceration, then a new device must be employed: poetic license. And that is exactly what Ai exercises in the Marilyn Monroe poem because, factually, Gladys Pearl Monroe, Norma Jean's mother, outlived her daughter by twenty-two years. In the poem, Marilyn stands over her mother's body dressed in her wedding gown, and then touches "the rhinestone heart pinned" to her blouse, "bright like the lightning" that killed her mother. The key to understanding the invented scenario as a metaphor is in the title, "She Didn't Even Wave." In the poem, Mama is upset about Marilyn's impending marriage and duly warns her: "*don't do it. / In ten years your heart will be eaten out / and you'll forgive him, or some other man, even that / and it will kill you.*" She storms out of the house and Marilyn is left pleading, "I've got to, Mama, / hug me again, please don't go." The invented scenario can be read as an amalgamation of a number of Marilyn Monroe's real-life dramas: her troubled relationships with men and the fact that her mother, mentally ill and in need of institutionalization, turned Marilyn over to the foster care system when the little girl was only seven. Though the poem attempts to show a contrasting representation of Marilyn Monroe in opposition to the glamorous sex symbol, the appeal remains Marilyn Monroe herself, who still overshadows the poetry because her darker moments are so public. There is little new to offer here.

Ai's more successful persona poems are those of the nameless and the downtrodden, even those who inhabit historical moments and social movements. She presents a human face (not always sympathetic, not always pleasant) to the experience by giving us these testimonies, such as the Nazi soldier in the poem "The German Army, Russia, 1943," in which, delirious with hunger on that ill-fated invasion, the soldier looks up at Hitler and imagines "eating his terrible, luminous eyes"; or the gay Jewish lovers, survivors of the Holocaust; or the Mexican revolutionaries, a deserter of Emiliano Zapata's army, a supporter of Pancho Villa's, loyal to a fault; or even Lope de Aguirre descending into madness in his search for El Dorado.

Killing Floor was just as well-received as *Cruelty*, and in this book Ai demonstrated an expansion of her territory—she would begin to populate her work with the named as well as the nameless. Still, the two poems that became instant classics were the ones that reminded readers and critics of the energy in her debut collection: "The Kid," about the young psychopath who bludgeons his parents, puts down the family horses ("Roses are red, violets are blue, / one bullet for the black horse, two for the brown.") and shoots his little sister while she's out playing in the truck. He packs a few personal items and sets off, coolly stating: "I'm fourteen. I'm a wind from nowhere. / I can break your heart." The other classic is "Lesson, Lesson," in which a man plays with his prepubescent daughter, plotting his victimization of her:

> Hear me. You imagine real good
> because your daddy a hammer.
> Hard-time nail in his pants.
> He feel wood beneath him,
> he got to drive it home.

One other poem worth noting is "29 (A Dream in Two Parts)." The numeral could easily be interpreted as twenty-nine years of age, which was close to Ai's age at the time of publication of *Killing Floor*—she was thirty-two. It's a rather cryptic piece, detailing two surreal moments, the second dream in which the speaker imagines herself *looking* at a nine-year-old girl and *being* that nine-year-old girl, is particularly fantastic. The poem is addressed to a "you," an adult, though that adult's relationship to the speaker is unclear. The only connection between the two dreams is a pair of hoop earrings: in the first dream the speaker is making them; in the second, the little girl is wearing them, though one comes off when she's held in the adult's arms. Sex is also prevalent: in the first dream, the speaker refuses to have sex with the figure that walks in naked while she's making the earrings and flatly states, "Do it yourself." In the second dream, as the speaker watches her girl-self in the adult's arms, she says, "Something warm seeps into my gown onto my belly." The poem ends with the assertion, "She never looks back."

Though the poem forces the reader to speculate about the dynamics at work, particularly if one imagines the adult to be a father, rather than a lover, there is little to support any specific argument (even whether that adult in the poem is a male). It's an odd situation because this poem is not as self-contained as some of Ai's other pieces, and also, there's little knowledge about Ai's personal life to place it within an autobiographical realm, which seems antithetical to the way Ai taught her readers to process her work. It's almost as if the message here is that she has hidden herself so deeply inside these constructed lives, searching for her is futile, even when she flirts with the notion of showing a part of herself by the way she has been revealing the intimacies and intricacies of others.

There was no contact between Ai and me until the year 2000, not long after Ai won the National Book Award. A friend of mine was working at the offices at W. W. Norton, which had published her volume *Vice: New and Selected Poems*, and when she gave me a photograph of Ai and her new home address in Stillwater, Oklahoma, I resolved to thank Ai by congratulating her on the award.

What happened next remains a point of contention between my friend and me: neither of us wants to take responsibility for me having addressed my letter to "Florence Anthony," Ai's birth name. But the blame, once Ai received the letter, fell entirely on me.

Though I had heard that Ai hated her birth name so much that she was known to kick correspondence all the way out of a building—a theatrical display of disdain—I seemed to have forgotten or never quite understood the extent of her deep-rooted rage against that name. I sent the letter, and within a week there was a message on my answering machine from Ai: *"Rigo, this is the poet Ai. I'm so glad you finally wrote, I was wondering when you would come around. Thank you for your letter, although, I was a bit surprised it was addressed to Florence Anthony—I mean, Florence is my given name, and Anthony was my father's name but—anyway, here's my number, why don't you give me a call?"*

I couldn't dial fast enough. I sat on the couch and heard the line ring a few times until she finally answered. What happened next is also a little fuzzy in my mind because I slipped into a state of shock: after her initial hello and repeating basically what she had said in the answering machine, Ai proceeded to berate me for the next fifteen minutes for having written to her and threatened the administrators at Norton for having released such confidential information as her home address.

What was running down my face didn't feel like sweat, it felt like blood because I became faint, frozen there with the phone pressed against my ear like a loaded gun. I suddenly realized I had pissed off the National Book Award winner, that whatever dreams of a career I had were getting shattered on that couch in New York City, just two years after I had arrived with two suitcases and a meager loan from my cousin in Seattle.

But then, just as unexpectedly as the cursing began, Ai's tone changed, for whatever reason, and her voice simply relaxed as she let out this phrase: "Well, anyway, enough of that. Let's start over. How are *you*?"

If I hadn't consumed *Cruelty* and *Killing Floor* I'm not sure I would have clung to the phone and followed her lead. Not that I was excusing her temperament, but somehow those books explained it. And perhaps out of guilt or perhaps because that's how she talked once she got going, she proceeded to unleash a mouthful, a monologue, not so dramatic, from the point of view of Ai.

I'm not certain how much time went by after exchanging those initial pleasantries (and their antithesis), but I held on to every piece of information since: Ai, who had never been able to score a permanent job, proudly stated that she had been made full professor with tenure at the University of Oklahoma after winning the National Book Award while she was visiting faculty there; she talked about how her date to the awards was a beautiful gay Native American—she *loved* gay men and was thrilled when she found out that the author of the book she had selected for the National Poetry Series (mine) was not only a Mexican from the Southwest, but also gay; she asked me to send her a copy of my book, not because she hadn't received a copy, but because she had sold her library when she made her move out of Arizona ("I needed the money. But now I don't need money and I want my library back. So I'll start with yours!"); she talked about the novel she was rewriting and about to finish, about the murder of her brother, how it would finally get published (though it never was); she asked me to send her my next manuscript and kept praising *So Often the Pitcher Goes to Water until It Breaks* because she loved its people and their "delightful, terrible stories."

Although we left off the conversation promising that we would seek each other out at the Association of Writers and Writing Programs' 2001 Conference in Palm Springs, I made little effort to look for her, apprehensive about whom I would actually meet. I was particularly vulnerable during that period, having just terminated a loveless relationship straight out of the pages of *Cruelty*, and having just moved out of New York City with no job and no direction, with only a series of invitations to read at colleges and universities across the country that would be my only source of income for the next six months.

I wasn't trying to avoid her at first but then I heard a rumor that she was looking for me. It was slightly off-putting, that phrase: *Ai is looking for you*. It sounded more like a threat. And then we ran into each other in the labyrinth of hallways at the conference hotel.

"Hey," she said, grabbing my arm. I was flattered that she even recognized me. "I have something to tell you, but I'm in a hurry, I have to be on this panel. I'll call you, okay, I'll find you."

That never happened. And the years went by without us crossing paths again. It was actually easy because the more she wrote about such public and well-known figures as JFK, Jr., J. Edgar Hoover, JonBenet Ramsey—figures from the popular culture and media that somehow seemed to intrigue and compel her to verse—the less visible and more withdrawn she became from the literary landscape. Her latest work was not receiving the critical acclaim of her earlier writing (the National Book Award notwithstanding), and it was clear that her persona poems were falling out of favor in an era where information was so easily attained, consumed, and spat out. With Wikipedia at one's fingertips, it seems that much easier and more sensible to plug into the fiction of cyberspace than into the imagination of poetry.

It's true that once a poet dies, readers freeze that poet's creative life at the height of the artist's popularity and power. With Ai, it's the 1970s, with a career nod to her contributions in 2000 by the National Book Foundation, which wasn't exactly a literary revival, though Ai managed finally to attain the financial security she was grappling with most all her adult life.

She remains, however, a mystery because in the age of networking technology and digital media, Ai resisted the spotlight, a reclusive, perhaps antisocial stance that today's writer cannot survive. I am certain she had a community, but I was not a member of it, or perhaps I was, but from a safe distance. I was only one of her admirers, a reader of her work, a poet who could claim her as a literary influence, a poet whom Ai championed at a critical time in his life. Without Ai, I am not sure where I would be today.

And if this is where I was meant to be all along, certainly the journey here would have been a much different one.

When the University of Oklahoma eventually posted an obituary on their website, it identified Ai as Ai Ogawa. Ogawa. That information was new to me and likely a choice made by the university administrators, not by the woman who clung so tightly to her two-letter name. But learning her adopted last name did little to unravel the mystery that was Ai. She left plenty of amusing stories to tell, plenty of poems to read, but she will remain, at least in my memory, that private woman with a penchant for sporting turquoise, who loved to browse through the shelves of the used book section, who poured all the chaos and noise onto the page so that she could have some peace and quiet in whatever unspeakable room she occupied.

Beloved Jotoranos

I will refer to my literary forefathers as *antepasados*, acknowledging the cultural connection of our shared Mexican (south of the border) and Chicano (north of the border) heritage. But I'd like to take it a step further, and recognize another important commonality: our homosexual identity. I will refer to my literary forefathers then, as *jotoranos*—my veteran queer godparents. These are the people who came before and who fought first, who braved the public stages and weathered the stormy audiences so that my own journey would be a little less terrifying and much more rewarding.

In this era where terms such as *post-racial* and *post gay* are erasing and disrespecting the scars and stretch marks of our ancestors' pasts, I feel especially compelled to thank these incredible teachers, mentors, and role models through the act of love I learned from them.

The seven thumbnail portraits that follow are only glimpses into the queer Chicano consciousness that has fueled my passion for the artistry and activism of language. Without them, there would be no me. Or rather, there would be a different me, less fulfilled and less skilled than the person who, through the works of these beloved jotoranos, has learned the pain of remembering, the pleasure of reading, and the responsibility of writing.

1. Arturo Islas

Arturo Islas died the day after Valentine's Day in 1991, almost a year after the release of his second novel *Migrant Souls*. News of his death was a particularly disappointing moment for me because I had resolved to attend Stanford University's graduate program just to work with him. I was only a junior at the University of California, Riverside, but I already had aspirations to become a writer. I had been reading Chicano literature voraciously, and one of the books that had moved me had been his *The Rain God* (1984). The sequel to the Angel family saga had just been released to wide acclaim and I spent the next twelve months fantasizing about telling Islas all about me. You see, the other thing I knew about him was that he was gay. A gay Chicano writer. Who knew there were two of us?

Miguel Chico, the college student who was hiding from his family by moving away, was someone I could relate to. I understood his bitterness over his invisibility, his dismay with the family dramas, and his heartbreak at the death of Uncle Felix, a cautionary tale of the dangers of homosexuality. And though Miguel Chico took a step back from the primary plot lines of *Migrant Souls*, he was still there, observing from a distance and trying to find a purpose for all of the knowledge he had acquired in school. I knew Miguel Chico's affliction, a melancholy that comes from loneliness and isolation, from breathing the same stale air inside the closet.

When I found out that Islas had died from complications related to AIDS I was devastated. This was not the narrative I wanted to follow—defeated by the very sexuality that was already making us foreigners in our communities. This was not supposed to be Miguel Chico's fate. Certainly not mine. But I accepted it as a reality of the times. It was a possibility that even literary icons could succumb to.

Suspending Miguel Chico at book two of a projected trilogy became a difficult state of incompleteness to inhabit. I wanted to find a light in his life that I could no longer see in Islas. I didn't know his happier memories because I never got to meet him. All I could do was piece together a fragmented portrait through his novels and through the snippets of information from his obituary.

His posthumous novel *La Mollie and the King of Tears* was published in 1996. It wasn't exactly the third book I had been expecting, but it did offer something else: a glimpse into Islas himself. The cool cat Shakespeare Louie, the protagonist of the novel, had a nutty teacher, Mr. Angel, who had a limp and a colostomy, just like Islas had. During one of his unconventional lessons, Mr. Angel comes to class wearing a woman's slip—his attempt at personifying a concept: a Freudian slip. Shakespeare Louie, jazz musician and lovesick vato from el barrio, actually becomes aroused watching Mr. Angel in drag. I was floored by this admission. Islas had somehow sexualized himself through his own characters by giving one of them permission to see past physical disability and to cross the border between gay and straight—transgressions without tragic consequences.

I felt that Islas had winked at me from the page, letting me know that it was going to be alright. That Miguel Chico, whether he had found happiness or not, had lived, loved, and been loved, and that was the important part of the story.

2. John Rechy

As a gay boy living in the pre-Internet era, I had absolutely no access to gay pornography. In fact, I didn't even have a home computer until I was twenty-eight years old. So before then, there was straight porn (magazines I would dig out from beneath the mattresses of any of the beds in the house) and the skin flicks of my mind—my adolescent fantasies. Thankfully, in college, there was a third option: John Rechy.

I first heard of Rechy while I was on a summer scholarship as a research assistant for an out-professor in the English Department, Gregory Bredbeck. At nineteen, I wasn't out of the closet on campus, but I suspected he knew and wanted me to know more. We were matched by accident and this turned out to be the best summer school I ever had.

My assignment was to seek out information for two of his projects. The first had me reading Elizabethan poetry with homoerotic overtones, such as the pastorals of Richard Barnfield, whose celebrated "Affectionate Shepherd" had me spinning because I knew what little pain and little joy doth awaited that shepherd boy! This material fed into Professor Bredbeck's scandalous book *Sodomy and Interpretation from Marlowe to Milton* (1991). The second project was a study on more contemporary homoerotic literature, so he thought it would be a great idea if I looked at the work of John Rechy.

I was stunned by the gorgeous photographs I found, many highlighting Rechy's trim and toned physique. I was intrigued by his middle name, Francisco, and that he had been born in El Paso, Texas. I was shocked by the details of his early life as a hustler—a fact that gave a startling authenticity to his works. But his vanity, his literary bravado, and even his name (his father was of Irish ancestry), are why he's been excluded from most Chicano or Latino literary canons.

Professor Bredbeck gave me a copy of *Bodies & Souls* (1983), and it became my naughty companion throughout many of my lonely nights in college. Eventually I read Rechy's classic *City of Night* (1963) and *Numbers* (1967)—amused by how many Chicano professors dismissed his work as pornography, and how I was employing the sex scenes as such, even as I objected to this unfair characterization.

I continued to read Rechy's works, especially after I became a book reviewer for *The El Paso Times*, which clamored for reviews of Rechy's books;

he was a native son and, coincidentally, the only other Chicano book columnist the newspaper had ever had. I reviewed (favorably) *The Life and Adventures of Lyle Clemens* (2003) and *Beneath the Skin* (2004), a collection of essays that gave me new insights into Rechy's politics and pride. He was a man of convictions—he despised the word "queer," he celebrated his Mexican ancestry, he wasn't ashamed of his past, of how he continued to hustle at night even as he taught writing classes by day at UCLA. Once he was standing, nice and oiled on a street corner, when a group of his students passed by in a car and yelled out, "Hey, professor, do you need a ride?" Such multilayered ironies were never lost on him.

Now in his late seventies, Rechy's still kicking. And I had a chance to meet him finally in 2008, when I was a faculty member for the Lambda Literary Foundation Queer Writers Conference. He showed up in a snazzy silver sports car and I was in charge of escorting him to the auditorium where he was going to give a talk. He chose the elevator because of his bad knees. And in that elevator I introduced myself again as the book reviewer for *The El Paso Times*. "Yes, yes, of course, I know you, Rigoberto!" he declared, and I beamed. At the end of his presentation, I rushed the stage to get my book signed first. I handed him a new edition of *City of Night* and a pen. He looked up at me, smiled, and asked, "What is your name, young man?"

I'm fine if Mr. Rechy forgets who I am. What's important is all the literary and masturbatory pleasure he gave to me. And Professor Bredbeck (who died in 2007 of AIDS at the tender age of forty-four), I will always remember.

3. Michael Nava

The name Michael Nava is inextricably bound to Henry Ríos. For the longest time I wasn't compelled to read his books because they were murder mysteries—a genre I loved but had outgrown by the time I started college. In my Chicano Studies classes his name wasn't mentioned even though he published five of his seven titles while I was earning my three degrees. My Chicano mariposa friends did know about him, though, and kept bringing up how cute he was and how charming that he was an activist lawyer who wrote books. I went to the local used bookstore and bought the book with the best author photo, a hardcover edition of *The Burning Plain* (1997). I also snatched up two paperback editions of *The Little Death* (1986) and *Goldenboy* (1988).

Before I made the big move to New York City in 1998, I drove my two cats and boxes of books across the California border, to my brother's house. And thereafter, every time I visited, I picked up a book or two to read on his lawn. On one occasion I devoured the Henry Ríos paperbacks, enthralled by the plots certainly, but also by the moral struggles of this regular gay guy who just wants to do what's right. It seemed unfair suddenly that Nava had been excluded from the reading lists of my education—my mariposa education. Here, finally, was a complex representation of a man whose inner demons had less to do with his sexuality than with the social fabric of truth and justice. But most importantly, Henry Ríos didn't define himself strictly through a single cultural lens—as either gay or Chicano—he was both. And he didn't qualify his profession through either identity because he was both.

It's important to note, however, that Nava is celebrated primarily by the queer literary community—the Chicano/Latino literary establishment has yet to catch up. I recall that back in 1997, while I was an artist-in-residence in celebrated Chicano writer Rudolfo Anaya's La Casita in Jemez Springs, New Mexico, my host was telling me he was going to establish a Chicano Mystery Writers Guild because they were growing (he was two titles into his own Sonny Baca series). When I asked him who would be invited, he listed Manuel Ramos, Rolando Hinojosa-Smith, and Lucha Corpi.

"That's four of us," he declared.

"What about Michael Nava?" I suggested. He looked at me blankly.

I'm happy to report, however, that in 2005, a teacher-scholar from Tucson, Arizona, wrote *Chicano Detective Fiction: A Critical Study of Five Novelists*. Without Nava's seven queer murder mysteries, Susan Baker Sotelo's analysis of Chicano literature's "21 whodunits" would be sadly lacking in scope and complexity. That same year, Brown University scholar Ralph E. Rodriguez released *Brown Gumshoes: Detective Fiction and the Search for Chicana/o Identity*, in which the works of the same five novelists (Nava, Anaya, Corpi, Hinojosa-Smith, and Ramos) are profiled.

Michael Nava and I had the opportunity to discuss these matters when we crossed paths three times within the same year in 2010—at the Association of Writers and Writing Programs Conference in Denver, at the Saints and Sinners Literary Festival in New Orleans, and at the National Association of Chicano Studies' Queer Conference (where I picked up the term *jotoranos* from the hip queer Xicano kids) in Eugene, Oregon, where he presented the keynote address, taking time out of his campaign. He wanted to be the first gay Latino judge to be elected in San Francisco. I congratulated him on all counts, reminding him that we needed him much more than he needed us. Unfortunately, Nava lost the run-off election with the incumbent judge Richard Ulmer. The final official vote was Nava with 82,100 (46.66%) and Ulmer with 93,869 (53.34%).

4. Richard Rodriguez

I'm detecting a pattern: Why are the mariposa writers not invited to the Chicano party? Of the four mentioned so far, Richard Rodriguez is probably the most embattled. To summarize: there was always a quiet politeness about Islas's sexuality—a don't ask, don't tell approach that basically closeted him all over again; Rechy was too "out there" for the curriculum reading lists; and Nava was never there. But Rodriguez continues to be Chicano literature's black sheep who betrayed la raza with his pen.

The book in question is *Hunger of Memory: The Education of Richard Rodriguez* (1982). Though this is an autobiographical account of one person's cultural displacement—surviving in an English-speaking world while living in a Spanish-speaking household—it has been held up as a go-to text that fortifies arguments against bilingual education or Affirmative Action. (Which is why Chicanos in particular—pro-bilingual education and pro-Affirmative Action—despise the book.)

In reality, the book is much more complex: it is about the negative conditioning and positive discipline that comes from being raised a Catholic; it is about the emotional and geographical distancing that occurs when a young man pursues a formal education and learns an academic language foreign to his parents, away from his parents; it is about loneliness. Sadly, both the pro- and anti-Rodriguez camps have pared down the text—a stylistically rich narrative—to a few vulgar catch-phrases.

The newer generations are not as invested in the fight. Partly because Rodriguez has since published two more books, *Days of Obligation: An Argument with My Mexican Father* (1992) and *Brown: The Last Discovery of America* (2002). In the pages of these books he softens his positions on language and identity because he has moved forward with the changes in society, such as the growth in visibility of Latinos in the mainstream media and culture and the awareness of the outspoken complex articulations against labels springing up from the postmodern *Generación Ñ*, which reconciles with language and heritage on its own terms. He's also become invested as a world citizen, bringing attention to the travesties of war as an appeal for US empathy and political responsibility through his journalistic profiles on *The McNeil/Lehrer NewsHour*.

Unfortunately, he has not been forgiven and his literary transgression has not been forgotten and his name opens deep-seeded wounds in the battle between assimilation and acculturation. I had the opportunity, over a period of two years (2002–2004), to converse with Richard about these and other matters. I didn't find the monster I was taught by my Chicano instructors to see. This had everything to do with the connection Richard and I had between us as gay men.

When *Hunger of Memory* was released, there were few clues about Richard's homosexuality. So when he was finally outed, Chicano scholars unfairly assessed what they called his "self-loathing" as the social anxiety of a closeted narrative. It became an easy way to explain away his conservative views and to alienate him—and his books—even further. Richard eventually comes out in his work, when he writes in "The Late Victorians" chapter of *Days of Obligation* about his loneliness as a gay man of color living in the Castro District of San Francisco. In *Brown* he goes a step further, writing deprecatingly about himself as an "old queen."

Our identities as gay men of color helped us reach past our differences and interact as intellectuals and as political beings. Richard was always flirty and witty (something I would have never guessed) but it was clear that he was still—despite his success and attention—lonely.

I remember at one point we were walking down Madison Avenue and the older Upper East Side crowd kept looking at us—at Richard. At first I took offense, but Richard simply shook his head and pointed out, "These people don't know me. They've never read my books. They just recognize me from TV." A few seconds later, they all turned their attention to an even bigger celebrity walking down the avenue: Sean Connery.

Richard and I exchanged a number of e-mails and phone calls during those two years, our gay repartée coloring the language a rosy pink. I was his Butterfly Boy and he was my Beloved Richard—we became a support group with its two members on different coasts. I called him when I entered rehab; he called me after his mother's funeral; I wrote to him after each breakup and heartbreak; he wrote to me after every trip abroad.

And just as suddenly as he appeared in my life he disappeared. This wasn't entirely unexpected. Richard is larger-than-life, a man of the world who travels solo because he carries a painful burden on his shoulders. Even the weight of one butterfly coming to rest on him would be too much to bear.

5. Salvador Novo

This story comes with a bit of drama. Back in 2002 I had an affair with a historian whose specialization was nineteenth-century México. We'll call him Víctor. Ours was an uneasy courtship because we tended to seek each other out when he wasn't single. On one of these ventures we met up in Mexico City, where we had a marvelous time exploring a number of historically significant sites. It was like sleeping with the city's most learned tour guide. Our bickering, however, was just as passionate as our love-making, and that particular rendezvous ended with Víctor dragging my suitcase out into the street, flinging it into the trunk of a cab, and slamming the taxi door in my face.

Such a backstory would have amused Salvador Novo without a doubt. In fact, he was the excuse we used to meet up in Mexico City. Víctor had been wanting to translate the works of Novo, especially his poetry, for some time. But he was not a poet, so he needed a bilingual one to move this project along.

I knew little of Novo except what Víctor told me: that Novo was a flaming, privileged dandy à la Oscar Wilde or Truman Capote, who was unafraid to write naughty poems about his fellow *bon vivants*; that he could write anything—plays, criticism, essays, memoir (he wrote the first gay memoir in Latin America in 1945)—and was considered to be the official chronicler of Mexico City (in 1967 he published a comprehensive study of Mexico City's culinary art). He died in 1974 at the age of seventy, and he had mentored, among others, México's leading gay intellectual, Carlos Monsiváis.

Víctor and I scheduled a meeting with Monsiváis (or Monsi, as he was affectionately called), to discuss how to proceed. I had already been taking a crack at translating a few of the poems and an essay, and Novo's work delighted me. It was so—for lack of a better word—fey. Novo loved beauty and luxury and wasn't afraid to appreciate it on the page without apology. He would write bold statements like "There have always been queers in Mexico" and back-handed verses like this poem dated October 2, 1915, which I translated. It is simply titled "For Salvador Guerrero":

> Oh, Salvador, you're so vindictive!
> And always so presumptive,
> that this morning, while I read,
> and while I schemed in bed,
> you, remembering my past offense,
> accused me to our Lord; I, left reprimanded

and bereft, but won't expect to be avenged
for vengeance, I hear,
is the vilest of weapons and for villains,
and double-edged, a spear
that wounds the avenger and not the object of revenge.
With a single forgiveness a thousand reprisals we avoid
and that is why I don't remain annoyed
with you. As proof of that I offer you my pardon.

Such fierceness strengthened my own resolve to introduce this incredible writer to English-reading audiences, especially my fellow mariposas. I was shocked that such a find, such a voice, had never been translated before.

After visiting with Monsi, we found out why Novo was never allowed to leave the country: it turns out that he had a dozen or so possessive relatives who refuse to grant anyone the right to translate without a generous compensation. And what's more, each of these relatives (none of them his direct descendants since Novo never had children) do not even speak to each other. So whoever deals with his work has to deal with each interested party's individual attorney.

Now, even Monsi is dead. And still Novo hasn't crossed the border. As for Víctor, I am happy to report that he has finally found a partner worthy of monogamy.

6. Francisco X. Alarcón

I have written about Francisco a few times before, but I didn't want to leave him out. Besides, I don't tire of it. Each time I sit down to write I think of something else worth remembering. On this occasion I would like to celebrate his untiring mentorship through poetry.

When I was his student at the University of California, Davis, back in 1993, he asked the literature class if any one of us wrote poetry. A few shy hands went up, including mine, although I was there to earn an MA degree in creative writing. He suggested that we get together once in a while to exchange poems and to learn from each other. I was so taken by the gesture that I began to think of these meetings as an important supplement to my graduate poetry workshops. Francisco always showed up smiling and he guided discussion so earnestly because he believed in us as poets.

One day he surprised us by inviting us to hear another group of students read poetry and that night we drove to nearby Sacramento where, unbeknownst to us, Francisco had been teaching a night class to a group of older folks. Gray-haired and wrinkled, their energy and love for the poem energized us. They invited us to read our own poems and some of us did. And then the audience clamored for Francisco to read one or two of his poems and he complied without hesitation. That's another thing I always admired about him: when he reads his work—columns in Spanish and English of two- or three-word lines that controlled his breathing all the way to the bottom of the page—it's always in the spirit of sharing not showboating.

I kept in touch with Francisco only through an occasional e-mail. He was gracious enough when he found out that my first column with *The El Paso Times* was a review of his book *From the Other Side of Night/Del otro lado de la noche* (2002), which included a number of homoerotic verses.

We ran into each other on the conference circuit. And in between those chance meetings I would hear reports that he was still fighting the good fight. I got to see another glimpse of that when he established a Facebook page in response to Senate Bill 1070, the Arizona law that allows racial profiling and the persecution of any person who looks Mexican. Francisco posts protest poetry submitted by anyone who is moved into activist verse. As a global forum it is attracting a sizable following. None of this surprises me. If any poet will make this place a better world it will be Francisco X. Alarcón, he of the contagious laugh and glorious ponytail, and a spirit with the scent of sage and copal. *¡Tahui!*

7. Gloria Anzaldúa

La mujer always has the last word.

On May 15, 2004, the day of Gloria's death, I lit a candle at my altar in my Upper East Side apartment and I read a few paragraphs of Chicano literature's most important book, *Borderlands/La Frontera: The New Mestiza* (1987). The wisdom of this woman's vision allowed many of us to find a place in our community—to reconcile our sense of disorientation with and our affection for our very own tormentors—our families. Before Gloria, the intersection of ethnicity and sexuality, of Chicanismo + queerness = jotería, had yet to take shape as a theoretical framework. We lived it but we couldn't quite articulate it within the lines of our poetry, the plots in our stories, the strokes of our paintings. She gave order to the chaos of our multiple planes of existence.

I left the candle burning and stepped out to grab a sandwich from the deli across the street. And during those brief fifteen minutes away, something—I have to say it—mystical happened to that candle. I came home to discover that the wax had splattered all over the wall as if someone had blown out the flame with an unrestrained force.

"Only Gloria," I muttered. Even her ghost had an untamed tongue.

I never had a chance to meet Gloria Anzaldúa, though I did have the opportunity to leave a sugar skull on her grave on the Day of the Dead.

November 2008. I was flying down to McAllen, Texas, to attend the wedding of a young Chicano poet, John Olivares Espinoza. I invited another Chicana poet, Emmy Pérez, to be my date since I was staying with her. It was she who suggested we make this pilgrimage to Gloria's grave. But first we decided to cross the Mexican border into Reynosa, where the Day of the Dead spirit was in full swing. The large sugar skull called to me and I thought it would be an appropriate gift for the woman who gave us borderland theory.

As I was walking back into Texas through customs, I didn't give the skull in my hand much thought, though this strange item did give the customs official, a young man in the trademark forest green migra uniform, pause.

"Excuse me, sir," he said. "What is that?"

I raised my eyebrows. "You're kidding, right?" I said.

The customs official was startled by my casual tone, though I really did think he was joking.

"I ask the questions around here," he said, scowling. "What's that made of?"

My jaw dropped. "Sugar," I said simply.

He was obviously Latino, his name tag confirmed it, and he worked here, on the border between the Day of the Dead and Halloween of all places, why wouldn't he recognize a symbol from either holiday? Additionally, my gaydar suddenly perked up, and though there really wasn't any way to confirm it I suspected that, surely, most likely, the dude was also queer. What was this show of power about?

And then I remembered Gloria. In fact, just like the candle wax blowing all over the wall, this had to be a message. No, the struggle is not over; yes, every minute means one more person to educate—especially, our own.

I stared at the customs official and though his face didn't change his eyes did. He was performing on many levels—as a border keeper, as a Homeland Security authority, as a human resisting the tugs of his private identities. Since this was his turf he was the one who broke the spell. He waved me through and focused his attention on the person behind me.

When I stood over Gloria's grave I didn't have to recount the story, it was all packed and pasted to the skull like the colorful swirls around the sockets. I placed the sugar skull on one corner of the large marble and granite tombstone—the largest in the small and humble cemetery of Hargill, Texas, where Gloria was also raised. Snakes had been carved into the face of the stone, and snake holes surrounded the grave.

My friend Emmy stepped away to let me spend some time with Gloria alone, and all I could think to say was, "I didn't get my entire security deposit back when I vacated that apartment in the Upper East Side, pinche. You left a permanent mark." I giggled and then I wept in gratitude.

Lullaby from Thomas James

1. Mr. Plath

There was something about Sylvia Plath that appealed to a young closeted farmworker kid like me back in 1988, my first semester in college at the University of California, Riverside, my first exposure to this huge presence in American poetry. That initial encounter was through an explication exercise in a composition class. The poem was "Metaphors." It sent my head spinning: nine lines, nine syllables per line, each line a dark glimpse into the nine-month condition I would never know—pregnancy. I bought Plath's Pulitzer Prize–winning *Collected Poems* soon after and I have been going back to this same copy since then, especially when I want to be dazzled by the two elements that continue to inspire my own writing: darkness and beauty. But at the time, I was less attuned to the craft and more sensitive to the current of emotional distress that unnerved the imagery; no matter how cool the delivery, the voice revealed ever so subtly a hint of anxiety and sadness. Yes, that was me in college, except that my own voice lacked strength and confidence. That would come later. In the meantime I was reaching out to the place I suspected I would find it—poetry—and to the person I knew would teach me—Plath.

In a predictable and unoriginal fashion, I began to dress in somber black, stay up until dawn, smoking cigarettes and sipping vodka, and associate with the only other people on campus who appreciated my clunky doomsday poetry—the Goths. This rather immature period of my life, unhealthy as it was, actually helped me come to terms with my sexuality. That inner peace was one of the few things (besides Plath) that I took with me to graduate school at the University of California, Davis, writing program. Soon after came *Letters to a Stranger*.

During my first year in the poetry workshop, my cohorts were kind and well-read, and they kept identifying the "Plath-swipes"—images I had plagiarized from Plath's better-known poems that I was claiming as my own.

One of them finally suggested: "You know, Plath is too much of an influence in your poems. Maybe you should stop reading her."

I bristled at the suggestion but conceded that if I wanted to move forward I needed to get off *Ariel*'s back. So I sought out other poets in an effort to break away from my obsession. And then by accident I overheard my poetry instructor say to another student: "Look up Thomas James. He's like, Mr. Plath."

I went into a tizzy. Though the comment hadn't even been directed at me, I gave myself permission to latch on to her advice. Suddenly it made sense that my instructor wouldn't make that recommendation to me because she too believed there was too much Plath already in my poems. In fact, she even admitted that she didn't particularly care for much of Plath's poetry, and as evidence of this she brought to class and read a copy of "Blue Moles" because it reminded her of something I had "swiped." She shook her head and quipped in the middle of the reading, "Sometimes I just want to take a pen to the page."

My instructor's criticism wounded me deeply, but I respected her opinion and deduced that this was her way of telling me to expand my narrow horizon. And there, by sheer accident, came my chance. I was determined to find Thomas James.

I suppose that initially, what I wanted in "Mr. Plath" was validation—if a published poet had been so influenced by Sylvia Plath then what was wrong with a mere novice exercising that same freedom? But even more than that I was in search of a kindred spirit, much like the ones I had as an undergraduate, ones I wasn't finding as a graduate student because the poets here were much older, more artistically certain, and less likely to explore the turbulent landscapes I was still inhabiting.

My search for *Letters to a Stranger* wasn't as fruitful as I expected. This was 1993, the era before Google, and e-mail was just starting to kick in. All I had were the old computers at UC-Davis with their glowing yellow script that told me the book, the only edition published by Houghton Mifflin in 1973, was out of print and unavailable, even through inter-library loan. I did, however, find a poem here and there through the forest of magazines shelved in the basement. The 1970 editions of *Poetry*, *The North American Review*, and *Poetry Northwest* offered up a few gems, and I thought it more than a coincidence that James's poems appeared in print the year I was born.

I copied and maintained a folder of James's poems, keeping my new obsession a secret, fearful that my cohorts or instructors would point out that I hadn't strayed far enough away from Sylvia Plath's backyard. Very quickly, James became as important to me as Plath, especially after I suffered my first nervous breakdown in graduate school after my entire family had decided to return to México after twelve years in California. They had asked me if I was coming with them, and I chose to stay alone in the country, to fend for myself with what little courage I had. James's poem "No Music" haunted me then, particularly the line "The dead have such sweet breath." As I plunged into depression and suicidal thoughts, I clung to the final stanza of that poem:

> It is impossible to move in all that white.
> Your face is a blossom thickening to anonymity,
> Erasing its features in a surge of downiness.
> One dark hand buds and loses its distinction.
> The light bruises and steps out of the room.

Somehow I survived my two years of graduate school, most likely because I didn't really want to self-destruct, I simply wanted to express it. And because I had no other destination after graduation, I decided to attend another writing program—this time as a fiction writer—at Arizona State University. As soon as I settled into my new home in Tempe, I marched straight to the library and looked for Thomas James. I knew I had made the right move coming to this state because lo and behold, thier library had a copy of *Letters to a Stranger.*

The back jacket bio read: "Thomas James is a twenty-six-year-old living in Chicago. He is the author of *Picture Me Asleep*, a novel that was dramatized by an experimental theater in the Chicago area." Ah, further connections: I had just turned twenty-four, I was almost the same age he was when he published this book! Ah, he also wrote fiction! And when I looked at the photograph—white turtleneck, a come-hither look coyly nesting among his long, delicate hair—I couldn't help but wonder: *And is he also gay?*

I photocopied the entire book because this was the only way I could possess it and caress it at home. I swam from cover to cover and back again, trying to find evidence of something deeper in his work, but I was still an amateur literary scholar so I didn't find proof of what I was looking for—that he, like me, was a homosexual.

Something else caught my eye, however. The dedication: "For my mother, 1912–1972, and my father, 1905–1972." Ah, yet another parallel between us, we were both without parents. My mother had passed away when I was twelve, and a few years later my father had abandoned my brother and me with our grandparents. Whether or not we shared the same sexual preference, Thomas James and I had so many things in common. I took solace in this as I read his poetry and wrote my own.

Eventually, the age of the Internet made finding lost loves that much easier. I was already living in New York City in 1999 when on a whim I searched for an old copy of *Letters to a Stranger*. I found one, selling for $150 from some bookstore in Minnesota. Though I had never purchased a book for such a price I knew it was worth it—James had been coming along for the ride all this time. But I also confirmed via some public cyberspace forum something I had heard rumors about—James's premature death by mysterious circumstances.

The death-wish was a condition I knew very well. Even while garnering modest literary success and a relationship with my first live-in boyfriend, I was still struggling with depression. That affliction fueled much of the affinity I had for Plath, James, and Anne Sexton. I wondered if James had entered that exclusive club through another experience: suicide.

When *Letters to a Stranger* arrived its brown cover made it look like a casket. The poem on page 53 resonated with the new information I had about James:

> I walked out hoping to evade redemption,
> The life I wanted to lose so badly
> Like an old wallet, a letter of introduction.

By then I had honed my skills as a critic and close reader, so I studied *Letters to a Stranger* yet again, this time with a more complete picture of the troubled artist who had written what I always considered to be an undervalued masterpiece.

2. Mr. James

The favorite word in *Letters to a Stranger* is "dark." The word or the ghost of the word inhabits nearly every poem. Yet it is expansive and all-consuming, enough to drape a sky and shroud a field, "putting the whole landscape to death." Light offers no respite because it simply illuminates other types of darkness—like a "blacksnake coiled in the berries" or the devil's granddaughter turning the rotisserie. And even if, with the arrival of light, there is a small consolation in identifying the shape and texture of the danger, light inevitably "steps out of the room" and leaves the body ringing inside another dark intensity—the speaker unsettled by the knowledge of the room's unsavory contents.

The dark rooms of Thomas James are metaphors for death—they are tombs, coffins—Sylvia Plath's pitch black, "So black no sky could squeak through." Sometimes this death comes quickly—the eyes slamming shut like doors—or it is a slow expiration, heavy with pain, as in the poem "Snakebite": "Out of the two red holes in my heel / Infinity pours, good-bye to all of me."

And, yes, even the humor is dark. In the poem "Head of Duck," a poor wounded creature walks right up to a house to take refuge from the rain and the family offers it a bed—the chopping block. But witnessing this decapitation gives the children nightmares:

> And, in waking, think of Mary Queen of Scots,
> Of Julien Sorel, Medusa's head,
> Louis XVI bleeding in the streets,
> And Herod's eyes as John the Baptist bled.

Poor little duck, that meal on webbed feet, unable to read the inscription on the doormat: "Abandon all hope, all ye who enter here."

This intimacy with the dead and dying, the suicide dreams and longing for death, the "poem spoken out of damaged lungs," is James's most apparent kinship with Plath. But these negotiations are much more internalized, while Plath's are performative and theatrical—"Lady Lazarus": "Gentlemen, ladies / These are my hands, / My knees." James's self-destructive speaker suffers alone, no one at the recovery room but himself: "They bring me the mirror— / I am thin and unshaven and even a little handsome."

And on the topic of recovery rooms, I can't help but notice the "Plathswipes" in James's "Room 101," which recall "The Stones" about "the city where men are mended" (part seven of Plath's "Poem for a Birthday"). At the end of this journey through the "head-stone quiet" where the "jewelmaster drives his chisel / to pry open one stone eye," the speaker in "The Stones" announces, "My mendings itch. There is nothing to do. / I shall be good as new." James's speaker is "chiseled out of the dark . . . My mended arms grow stiff and lean. I come to trade my flesh for stone." And later: "My new stone biceps itch."

As another point of comparison, I am reminded of Plath's poems to poppies while reading James's poem "Peonies." For Plath, the "little hell flames" igniting the carbon monoxide are the "late mouths" crying open for attention in a forest of frost; for James, the red is "frightening," it is "like opening an artery." His flowers do not cry as much as the witness to their fury: the peonies "bloom like a cancer / Eating the heart out of this room."

This familiar suffering from within is what attracted me to James, and because he was male, I recognized that he was breaking a taboo of masculinity by expressing pain, vulnerability, and weakness. Could there be something else cloaked by those words? Could I, should I, read between the lines of those letters to a stranger?

The poem "Hunting for Blackberries" gave me pause, with its confessional narrative in which the speaker admits to a questionable relationship with an eight-year-old blind cousin: "My hands were two large spiders that reached your bed / Each night." Comparing the speaker's grip to that of a python's and the subsequent introduction of a snake about to strike, only loads the poem with sexual, predatory imagery, identifying the speaker as a male. Though the gender of the child is never revealed, this doesn't matter because the poem is not about sexuality but about abuse. Yet somehow, perhaps because it seemed unlikely that a blind girl would be in the care of an older male cousin, I deduced that the younger cousin was also male. As a gay man myself, I want to tread carefully and not confuse homosexual tendencies with molestation, but this poem stands out early in the collection as the one with the more explicit and sexually charged subject matter. It is more of a clue than an admission to anything and an oddity among the numerous persona poems and dramatic monologues in which the speakers suffer and ponder their self-inflicted pain. It is a poem without disguise—has another dark room been lit?

And then the book comes to a close with another oddity, the poem "Reasons," whose second-to-the-last line inspired the title of my second collection of poetry, *Other Fugitives and Other Strangers*. I read and re-read this piece and it finally dawned on me that it was nothing less than a cruising poem—an account of the anonymous sexual encounters between men in a public park that take place in the cover of night:

For our own private reasons
We live in each other for an hour.
Stranger, I take your body and its seasons,
Aware the moon has gone a little sour

For us.

...

I am aware of your body and its dangers.
I spread my cloak for you in leafy weather
Where other fugitives and other strangers
Will put their mouths together.

Suddenly, the interiority of Thomas James took on another dimension and I began to read other pieces through a different lens, like the poem "Cold August" about two people who make love in silence, in the dark, their love-making a transgression that dares not speak its name:

But soon their footsteps break across the doorway,
Leaving the clock behind. They shape no words,
But force their eyes into the vicious day
Against the sudden flight of hungry birds.

I didn't confirm that Thomas James was gay until September 2008, when I spoke at a presentation at The New School, presided by the author of the new edition's introduction, Lucie Brock-Broido. She also revealed to us his real name: Thomas Bojeski. Thomas Bojeski—the layer beneath the layer—a figure with much to explore and discover. So, I had only been grazing the surface all along with my inklings and suspicions that buried underneath the tight-lipped rigidity of a Plath-like language was another demon being wrestled.

Perhaps that's why I was tickled to come across the poem "Tom O'Bedlam Makes Love," one of the newly discovered pieces in the new edition of *Letters to a Stranger*, because it uncovered a more playful, naughty Thomas James I knew was just screaming to come out. This little poem about masturbation contains the lines:

Inside me, locked up in a tiny cell,
The devil hides himself. He is a ripe volt waiting,
He is a yellow dwarf with ragged nails,
Waiting. I am his warden. I own the key.
One click and he is eating his way out.
My penis sings like a tuning fork.

O my love I am a slide trombone
When I slide into you. I am matches to your straw.

3. Mr. Bojeski

So where to next, Thomas Bojeski? In September 2007 I wrote a brief appreciation of *Letters to a Stranger* on Harriet, the blog of the Poetry Foundation, because I had just heard from Mark Doty that Graywolf Press was reprinting it in the Re/View Series. Doty also invited me to participate at the panel/book launch at the Association of Writers and Writing Programs' 2009 Conference in Chicago, where a classmate of Thomas James identified himself to the stunned presenters. I am not sure, however, that the new generation of angst-ridden poets, particularly gay ones, will be as drawn as I was to James and his formalist and coded sensibilities from the late 1960s.

The release of the new edition of *Letters to a Stranger* was a gracious gift to James's fans, and though there was initial buzz about the book it will most likely be prized as yet another relic of the troubled lineage of "confessional poetry." It is now readily available nonetheless, and, however a reader comes to the book, he or she will no longer have to piece together the narrative of Thomas James's life and poetry the way I did, over the course of fifteen years.

Where to now? To bed. To the one I hope to wake up in after a restful or restless sleep. Sometimes these things are out of my control. Yet what is always there is a book next to the pillow. Tonight the poem "Letters to a Stranger" sings to me its peculiar yet beautiful lullaby, cooing the words I want to breathe back into Thomas James's ear:

> All the while I am thinking of you.
> An avalanche of white carnations
> Is drifting across your voice
> As it drifts across the voices of confession.
> But the snow keeps whispering of you over and over.

Roxana's Melody

1.

Behind me, my father says, *Súbele, Mija*
and rocks us both back,
to my first dancing lessons
when I could hear the Lava Soap
scrubbing engine grease off his hands
before he slicked his hair back
with water and a pocket comb.
Then, I would spin away
from El Camino on cinder blocks
and into his aura of Old Spice.

—*"Dancing Lessons"*

Roxana Rivera was introduced to me in the spring of 2002. I usually flew into Los Angeles for Thanksgiving to celebrate with my good friend Maythee Rojas, whom I refer to as my sister—her family now my family. Maythee had invited me to partake of chompipe (what Costa Ricans call the turkey) with her small four-member, all-female household back in 1994, when we were both penniless graduate students at Arizona State University, and we have kept that tradition sacred since then. But on this occasion I happened to drop in on Maythee in the spring. I held a visiting appointment at The New School in New York City, and Maythee held a teaching appointment with the Women's Studies Department at Cal State, Long Beach. Roxana was one of her undergraduate students. And a poet.

I didn't like to be introduced to young poets. At thirty-one, I was just beginning my own journey so I felt like a young poet myself with little knowledge of the mysterious workings of the literary field. My first book had only been out in the world a few years, but that still didn't endow me with any special insights. At least that's what I claimed. The truth was that I was extremely anxious about being considered a role model let alone a mentor. It seemed premature. I had yet to overcome my stage fright or learn to disguise my awkward shyness. When I wanted to exude confidence I came across as haughty.

Thinking back on that lunch in Long Beach, when I agreed reluctantly to meet Maythee's protégée, I can only imagine what a first impression I must have made. The day was too warm, I wasn't dressed for the weather, and I sat sweating on an uncomfortable aluminum chair of that trendy outdoor café with its over-priced chicken salad. Roxana was about twenty-five years old, so she was a little older and more mature than most undergrads. Her hair and makeup were impeccably done and she exuded a strength and femininity that I appreciated in women like my sister Maythee. I could see why they were drawn to each other.

"Who do you read?" I asked Roxana.

"Sandra Cisneros, June Jordan, Lucille Clifton, Audre Lorde," she said and I smiled in approval.

"Any other Chicanos?" I asked, taking a sip of my iced tea.

"I like Lorna Dee Cervantes and Luis Rodríguez," she said. She then added with an air of determination: "And I read your book. I liked that too. That's why I want to talk to you. I want to go to an MFA program."

Maythee had explained to me that although Roxana could be a valuable feminist scholar, she would be happier as a writer. She had been taking writing classes with the poet Lisa Glatt and had been talking about applying to the writing program at Southern Illinois University, Carbondale, where she could work with another poet she admired, Allison Joseph. My task, should I accept it, was to guide her through the process—giving her advice on application materials, and feedback on the creative writing sample and the personal statement.

"Why don't you send me a few poems," I said to Roxana, but with reservations. I had been through this route before: encountering young people with all the hunger and ambition and not much of the talent. Fortunately, that was not the case with Roxana.

Over the next year we corresponded very little over e-mail, but I knew she was multitasking: finishing up her Women's Studies degree and polishing her poetry. We had a few conversations over the phone—pep talks about overcoming the frustration of revision and other writerly matters. Without verbalizing it, I had become her mentor and I was taking the role seriously. There were two other young writers I had been advising from afar: California poet John Olivares Espinoza and Arizona poet Eduardo C. Corral. I encouraged all three to attend the Association of Writers and Writing Programs Conference in Baltimore. John and Eduardo knew each other, but neither had met Roxana. I thought it would be an appropriate place to close the circle and to connect Roxana with her Chicano writing community. I even paid for a second room at the conference hotel, where Roxana stayed with two other Chicana writers, María Meléndez and Diana López, on tight budgets; the guys and I jokingly called it "The Women's Shelter."

February 2003 in Baltimore was the second-to-the-last time I saw Roxana. She had submitted her graduate program applications and was now waiting to hear back, though I already knew from the program administrators at Southern Illinois that she would be hearing good news from them. It was at this conference that she met her future mentor, Allison Joseph.

Exhausted from the crowded hotel elevators and hallways, I took my three charges out for lunch on that day. I bought a silly hat shaped like a red crab for Roxana to deliver to Maythee on her trip back to Los Angeles, and then we walked along a pier covered in snow and told dirty jokes in Spanish until we couldn't stand the cold any longer. It was at that moment that I realized with a combination of fear and pride that this was my calling: looking out for the talent that I could nurture. On the way in, they all thanked me for lunch, but I reminded them: "Don't thank me today. Thank me tomorrow when you can do this for someone else."

At the end of the conference, we said our good-byes, everyone going back to their respective homes in the Southwest. I would be coming through Los Angeles again later in the summer, I told Roxana, and I promised to come by and visit.

When I finally made my way to Los Angeles again, Roxana was already planning her move to Carbondale, Illinois. Maythee told me her family was sad to see her move so far away, but that they were supportive. They did, however, want to meet me, this "poet-guy" who had filled their "poet-girl" with these crazy ideas about becoming an artist.

Maythee and I attended a small party in the Rivera household, where Brenda Rivera—Roxana's younger sister—was celebrating the completion of an educational endeavor. Maythee and I watched with amusement as Brenda handed out Certificates of Appreciation to her parents, her grandmother, her neighbors, and to Roxana.

"I hope she goes through with it," I whispered to Maythee. Watching the closeness of this family made me worry that at any moment Roxana or her parents, confronted with the reality of the separation, would have a change of heart.

"Are you kidding?" Maythee said. "They're making a road trip out of it. Everyone's coming along, including the grandmother. Maybe even the dog."

The DJ started spinning dance music and Maythee and I thought it was the appropriate time to sneak away. The last time I saw Roxana, she was dancing in her father's arms.

2. The Xicana in the Mirror

Roxana Rivera was proudly a Chicana from LA, born in Monterey Park and raised in Lynwood, the oldest of three sisters, the daughter of a postal worker and an employee at the Los Angeles County clerk's office. The working-class urban landscape and its troubling imagery featured prominently in her poems, such as in "Drop," which speaks to the tragedy of gun violence and how anxiety embeds itself into the community's consciousness:

> They shot a boy in my driveway.
> I woke up to my sister screaming
> *Call 911—DROP!*
>
> Drop: the one word in our town
> that means death, rage, bullets, cop.

And in a companion poem, "In Concrete," which references the same scene, Rivera offers a glimpse into the act of healing and closure via an altar erected over the place of bloodshed. For the grief-stricken and shell-shocked alike, this ritual imbued with religious symbolism is essential for survival:

> Death becomes a chicken heart stuffed
> with pennies tonight, thrust down my throat
> as strangers surround the candles
> lighting a corner of my driveway beside roses,
> carnations and pictures of a boy nobody
> on my block knew.

Though the landscape of Rivera's poetry is fraught with threats ("aluminum signs blaring out *keep out* in Old English lettering") and danger ("I buzzed high on fear, / like the first time I heard your father / put his fist through the door"), the female speaker finds power in the two emotional centers she keeps sacred: a love for her ancestry and an appreciation for her femininity.

The poem "Trenzas" celebrates the connection of language, culture, and gender between a granddaughter and her Abuelita from Juárez who, at ninety-eight, still cares for her braids. But in the poem, which features a hair salon, a kitchen, and a bedroom with a religious altar, the grandmother doesn't remain confined to enclosed domestic spaces, she's also capable—through the speaker's dream—of becoming the granddaughter's sister, the two women breaking-in horses, drinking at the campfire, and wearing "an X of bullets across our chests / [as] we burn amber points in a haze of cigar smoke."

The women are not being masculinized as much as they are re-inscribed into a historical space (the Mexican Revolution) that has been claimed by men but factually experienced by both men and women—las soldaderas. This legacy of woman strength is what the speaker continues to access even after Abuelita is gone:

> I look beneath my bed for her braids before I sleep
> to feel the ripple of a rosary and horse whip,
> to catch the scent of river-water and blood,
> to steal her hair away from the linoleum's corners.

La soldadera spirit is a manifestation of the self, "the Xicana in the mirror" that nurtures the female speaker's agency and visibility. It is sought, through the same act of narrowing the generational distance between a girl and (in this case) a picture of her "mother's grandmother," in a second poem, "El Árbol":

> She hides
> my destiny, I think. I want to dissolve the glass
> and decades, to pull 50 years off her face
> and see my own every time I feel the warm hole
> of love oozing inside me.

The Xicana in the mirror, "armed" with confidence and knowledge—or at least the certainty that such intangibles are available and attainable—

navigates through the sentiment of other poems. In "*¿Cómo Se Dice?*" (with its politicized dedication—"for the pocha poets everywhere"), the speaker shifts from a shaky flirtation with a man who speaks perfect Spanish into a self-assured stance—her seduction fortified by her belief that her code-switching is an unassailable and legitimate language.

The Xicana in the mirror thrives in her multiple tongues and in her disparate settings: she can stay up until two in the morning to sing (in the poem "Winters") "bi-lingual duets into a hairbrush" with her Mexican prima, or she can walk (in the poem "Vertigo") into a "lounge where leopard print couches pulse against velvet walls," attracting boys with "the swing of my hips or the click of stilettos."

In essence, a Xicana's place is any space she can imagine or inhabit but this is not achieved without conflict or struggle, therefore Rivera gives her Xicana yet another avenue for expression and introspection—poetry ("the flood of words and voices / that pours onto a page at dawn / helps this story breathe"). In "Last Calls Echo Loudest in Empty Houses," after a "night of cigarettes, sex / and beer," the speaker processes the bodily pleasure and emotional pain of confusing lust with love. She recalls the bliss of an earlier sexual encounter and situates the relationship within the creative power and control of her memory and poetry:

> When last calls echo through my house,
> I wrap myself in that morning.
> Nestled in my bed sheets,
> I want to take back the sonnet
> I tore out of a book, slip my number
> into his jacket and feel his lips kiss
> my thighs as he says, *Read me your poems.*

This brief study would be remiss if Rivera's most beloved poem "Tita's Soto" was not mentioned. This prose poem brings together elements I have already highlighted and so it is an appropriate place to conclude.

Soto is the East LA street where this particular photograph was taken: the speaker wearing "Barbie panties" and licking a paleta de coco that's melting into streams of ice cream on her exposed belly. The toilet turned flower pot in Tita's garden speaks to Tita's working-class ingenuity; the sávila plant next to the kitchen window is a symbol of old México and folk medicine. But when the speaker reveals that this picture on her nightstand has been stolen, she acknowledges the sentimental value placed on the memory of Tita's affection and watch over the vulnerable girl who now "takes" what is rightly hers: the past, the land, the nurturing spirit, and the creative drive. But most importantly, family and community—the courage to leave it behind and the knowledge to find her way back: "I'll lie awake waiting for the neon Sears sign to light up and tell me which way is home"

3.

> Burgundy helmet—
> perm stays still as Tía shakes
> her head asking my
> mother, "Four years of college,
> no husband, and she's happy?"
>
> —*"Tanka"*

Roxana began her graduate studies at Southern Illinois University in the fall of 2003. I made it a point to check in at least once a month. But she was thriving—her personality quickly made her a popular member of the program. Roxana was very unlike me that way—she was not shy and she did not suffer from stage fright, her signature boot steps always announcing her arrival with purpose. On our final phone call in November, we made plans: I wanted her to come to New York City and fall in love with Manhattan the way I had. Next summer would be perfect; I would be gone to Scotland for a month. When I mentioned that I'd be in California over the winter she interjected, "So will I! Let's go dancing!" She was excited about her writing, she was excited that she had been invited to be a presenter on a Chicana poets panel at the next AWP conference in Chicago. I was excited for her.

"So everything's fine? You're happy?" I said as a way of concluding the conversation.

"Yes, everything's fine. And how about you, Rigo?" she said, her voice becoming coy. "Any news from the love department?"

Roxana knew this kind of talk made me blush, and as I felt my cheek growing warm next to the cell I could hear her giggling. "Cómo eres," I said.

A week later, on November 21, my poet-girl Roxana was killed in a single-vehicle accident. Maythee called with the news, delivered in a fit of tears. I responded in kind and made incoherent phone calls to a few close friends, to Allison Joseph, to Roxana's mother. I was suddenly consumed with an unshakable guilt about having ushered her toward the place that would end her life. It was illogical, but it felt heavy and real. "She died doing what she loved," Roxana's mother said to me by way of comfort. But it wasn't enough.

I carried this burden with me on the flight to California to attend Roxana's funeral, where the many communities of Roxana's life clustered into a single trembling mass. At church and at the cemetery I separated myself from the others. We had all lost Roxana in our individual ways but I could only deal with mine: my poet-girl was gone.

I had a visceral response to Roxana's death. I had placed such high expectations on this young talent—I was certain that she was going to be "the one." She was going to succeed—she would have seen to that. Her death sent me spiraling into a depression I had only experienced once before, when my mother died in 1982. And yet, I had only known Roxana for a little over a year.

While in residence at Hawthornden Castle in Scotland the following July, I celebrated my thirty-fourth birthday partaking of a quiet toast with the other residents. I thanked them and retired to my room. I stayed up until four in the morning, listening to the sounds of the forest just outside my window. And then I heard a strange shrieking, a wounded animal that in its pain was actually drawing attention to itself. I expected the creature to stop making noise at any second, silenced by the arrival of a predator. But the shrieking did not cease for the next few hours. It was as if instead of provoking temptation it had provoked sympathy and the inhabitants of the forest let the cry run its course. The sound eventually faded—the animal grief tapering down to nothing, like a heartbeat slowing to a stop. I grabbed a pen and paper and I picked up where that sound left off, writing a poem in remembrance of the poet who wrote the following lines about the continuity of the world and the word:

> We are all one flute
> in a long line of reeds and pipes
> silenced and pitched
> by the submission of a muse,
> or a breath of Coatlicue
> carried in a southern wind.

Speeches

To the Writer, to the Activist, to the Citizen

Note: The National Latino Writers Conference (NLWC) held its first formal meeting in 2003 and is the only national writers conference to tailor its workshops and panel discussions exclusively for a Latino audience. The conference is sponsored by the National Hispanic Cultural Center in Albuquerque, New Mexico, and is under the direction of Carlos Vásquez. Mr. Vásquez invited me to be the keynote speaker at the eighth annual meeting and I immediately accepted: trouble was already stirring (yet again) regarding immigrant issues, this time in Arizona, with the introduction of Senate Bill 1070. Spear-headed by Governor Jan Brewer, this contentious policy would require officials and agencies of the state to assist in the enforcement of federal immigration laws. As a person of Mexican descent, it's difficult not to feel personally assaulted by these hostile policies that purport to distinguish undocumented immigrants from the rest of the Latino population—a miraculous feat indeed, how can anyone tell one brown face from another? At the national level, this and other affronts helped energize a community (particularly young people) that had grown steadily apathetic and apolitical since the Chicano Movement of the 1960s. As a writer and intellectual, I could only respond the way I knew—through the written word. The first effort was a posting in April 2010 on the Poetry Foundation's online blog, Harriet—an essay titled "Boycott Arizona," which drew plenty of support and, not unexpectedly, hate mail. The second effort was drafted a few days later as the following keynote address, which was meant to inspire and politicize Latino writers at the NLWC. It was well received and widely disseminated through the Internet. Called a "Latino writer's manifesto" by some, it is also a celebration of agency: we will not be defeated by acts of violence and hatred against la raza, we will be empowered by them. Three years later, the sentiment behind this speech still stands, because the Mexican/Chicano/Latino community continues to be at the receiving end of policies designed to convince us that we are an inferior people. We are a fierce people, and we are feared because we are many and quickly multiplying. We are threatening because we are inevitably the future leaders of this country.

May 10, 2010

Before I begin I would like to thank the organizers of the National Latino Writers Conference for inviting me to participate this morning as the keynote speaker at this exemplary gathering. This event marks another year of building community, of fostering creativity and critique, and of guiding early-career writers toward mentorships and professional relationships with established writers whose generosity and insights are shaping the next generation of artists. To be honest, there is nothing unusual about these expectations at any writers conference, and there are dozens that take place across the country—most of them perfectly competent and useful. But what makes *this* conference so unique is that it is ours—a forum that has facilitated the face-to-face communication between *Chicana/o and Latina/o* writers, readers, and thinkers. And for that, I congratulate all of you who have sacrificed time and resources to contribute to that experience.

We are currently standing beneath the shadow of the anti-immigrant and anti-raza legislation of our neighbors in Arizona (and let us hope that the disease of xenophobia is not contagious), but I am going to keep my message positive because, despite these acts of hostility against our people, there is much for us to celebrate. And if we do not recognize our successes, if we do not toast our triumphs, then we surrender to the afflictions of inferiority, invisibility, and silence—the three disgraces of American politics and culture.

Behind us we have the 2010 US Census, which has confirmed for the country what we have always known when we wake up in the mornings to see the Aztec sun casting its rays over Aztlán: that we are plentiful, that we have always been here, that we are never leaving, that we will *not* be thrown out. In front of us, we have the smoky memory of revolution, the cycle comes back to the days of reckoning—1810, 1910, 2010—though all along and long before we have been populating this land, we have also shaped its language, built its cities, spun its tales, and written its songs. This is, indeed, nuestra tierra and we will keep the roots of our family and history embedded deeply into its indigenous and mestizo core.

But now come the important questions: How will each of us accept that responsibility? How will we contribute to this movimiento during this critical period of adversity? How will we know that we are marching on the correct path?

Because I am speaking to a group of poets and writers, I will speak to the answers through a cultural lens, acknowledging one of the greatest strengths of our community: its artistic muscle. Art and poetry, danza y teatro, cuento y canto, have always been essential components of the Latino cultural identity. From the pachanga navideña to the quinceañera, from the floricanto to the academic encuentros, we express ourselves through the arts because it is who we are: people who value creativity and imagination. Just look around you: the colorful palette of our folklore, the ingenious architecture of our altars, the linguistic textures of our slang, our names, our adivinanzas, the panoramic flavors in our foods, the range of decibels in our music, our cyber-chisme, our rascuachismo—*please*, somebody send the memo to Governor Jan Brewer: we are here to stay!

The impulse to dance and sing and, yes, the impulse to write it all down, to record and remember, is as natural and familiar to us as the impulse to breathe. And it is with great urgency that we need more of that breath.

There has been much to-do about how Chicana/o and Latina/o writers are now getting their due, getting their props for their hard work, getting published more, and winning more awards. And yes, all of those points of progress are true and they are real. And they are ours. Yet, if we allow those statements to settle without further examination, it would appear that only until recently have we discovered our talents. Or rather, that only until recently have we been discovered, which is to say, only until the white industries and institutions saw us did we see ourselves.

Let us not drop into the pitfall of charting our history and our territory using the maps and timelines of those who came to *our* neighborhoods long after the ink had dried on *our* pages. If we accept those observations as facts, we neglect the labor of previous generations of writers who produced and didn't get published in venues of high visibility, who shared and didn't garner those accolades, who educated and were not memorialized. I find it hopeful that we have many more opportunities to spread the word, but I will find it shameful if we move forward as if we had invented that word. So let us speak frankly about where we are now, by first paying tribute to those who paved the way toward the privilege of authorship and of organizing literary gatherings like this one, the National Latino Writers Conference.

If we learn anything from this recent bout of American societal anxiety, it is that numbers don't signify safety or acceptance or victory. In New York City, in the place I now call home, Mexicans will outnumber Dominicans and Puerto Ricans by the year 2025. By the year 2050, Latinos will outnumber all other minority groups in the country. You would think that this relatively quick population explosion—indeed the browning of the United

States of America—would also translate into population explosions in other areas, such as education and the arts. It will only seem that way because of the social networking media and technology that allows us to connect with other artists with a speed and efficiency that has never been experienced before. The truth is there will not be more of us, we will only be more aware of who and where we are. Only by choice will an artist remain detached or isolated, only by choice will a poet or writer remain disconnected from a literary forum. I say this as both an advantage to the young talent aiming to see itself as part of a bigger picture, as well as a disadvantage resulting in a skewed perception: there are not more of us and our numbers as artists, compared to our ethnic population, is and will remain devastatingly small.

This might sound like a contradiction to what I pronounced earlier, that the arts were the vibrant fabric of Latino cultural identity—but it is not a contradiction, it is complexity, and I'm referring to the specific representation in letters. Instead let us look at this as a challenge: and that challenge is in sustaining and empowering the writer. If we do not build, now that we have the tools, a system of nurturing and professionalizing the young writer, we will lose that writer, we will lose a warrior in the battle of the word against inferiority, invisibility, and silence.

So let me now pose the following points as a framework of responsibility to all of us inhabiting the Chicano/Latino literary landscape. This framework is a strategy for survival if we are to move ahead into the new millennium as champions of our own cause. It's actually a simple formula, but a hard one to achieve without the collaborative energy to fuel it. This two-point prong is mentorship and community.

For the young members of our audience: learn who your literary antepasados are—know their names and read their words. This will keep your humility in check and your esteem on fire. Recognize that your influences are from a variety of bookshelves, not just writings from Chicana/o and Latina/o writers, but also the writings from our Latin American cousins, plus the works in translation from Africa, Europe, and Asia. Embrace your town or village or city but locate it within a larger map—world literature.

Never be ashamed or embarrassed to call yourself a Latina/o writer. In fact, be more specific, call yourself a Chicana/o writer, a Dominican writer, a Puerto Rican writer, a Cuban American writer, or any configuration or combination of these and other identities. Situate yourself within a nation and an immigrant history, that is what preserves the integrity of the sacrifices of your people and the loss of your people's homeland. I'm frequently dismayed by Latina/o writers who subscribe to the notion of wanting to "just be a writer, not a Latina/o writer," as if that designation "Latina/o writer" wasn't true. Unless you don't carry any signifier of ethnicity in your name, unless your work doesn't illustrate your cultural identity, unless you can pass for white, you will never be "just a writer." By moving forward with this delusional goal you are betraying your own inferiority complex, you are buying into the stigma imposed by the mainstream publishing industry that you are lesser than, regional, foreign, and derivative. This is why you need to read your literary antepasados—so that you can navigate the troubled waters of doubt, writer's block, or other creative frustrations with the strength and pride of those who came before you.

For those of you who have already started publishing or who are in the early stages of a career, those of you who have one or two books under your belt, don't rest on your laurels and expect the readers to come to you. Take some initiative and become your own best advocate: learn to speak in public, to articulate matters of craft and all things literary. You learn these skills by attending readings and listening to seasoned voices, by attending conferences such as this one and absorbing the wisdom, advice, and knowledge of your instructors. Recognize that even at this level you have something to teach others—share your mistakes *and* your moments of success. And don't forget, as you further your career, that you are more than "just a writer." You are also a role model: take responsibility for your public appearances, choose your words carefully, and fight with intelligence—you are now a public figure, generate praise for those who are your colleagues not your competition, and don't become that writer who chooses to remain detached or isolated, who chooses to remain disconnected from any literary forum. That sidestepping of accountability to your artistic community is nothing short of selfishness. Such weakness is the weight around the necks of the rest of us who must pull forward a little harder because *you* won't.

You are a Latina/o writer, so you are also an empowered voice: speak out through your poems, through your stories, but also through editorials and informed opinions. Write those essays or blog entries, those words of critique and protest. Become politicized because writing is political, Latina/o identity *is* a political stance. Have you not heard that "breathing while brown" is the latest oppression? Or are you "just a person" as you are "just a writer"? Being afraid is no longer an excuse, it's a surrender. What use is our growth in numbers if we start censoring our language, tempering our tones, and apologizing for our passions, our outrage, and our cries for justice? We cannot hide behind the politeness of our advanced degrees or beneath the decorum of art spaces. Avoid the trapping of early success, called complacency, and tell yourself that if you don't rock the boat you will be fine. Cowardice is never rewarded. Writing is not a static activity, it is activism. Learn it and then teach it to others.

For the veteran writers in the room, I know you have journeyed far and labored tirelessly all these years, well, I am now asking you to work harder by keeping the doors you kicked open cleared for the rest of us. Too many times I have heard the doors slam shut as soon as one of us makes it in. Fortunately, there are many members of this elite group who mentor, who write reviews and endorsements on book jackets, who write letters of recommendation and academic evaluations, who introduce younger writers to publishers, editors, agents, and other writers. To those people I say thank you, and may you continue to do what you do best and what we appreciate.

The tragic side of that coin is that there are writers who do not contribute to the efforts of mentorship, who guard their writing time so jealously they see the rest of us as termites who will chew through the walls of their writing rooms if they even acknowledge us. They shall remain nameless, and may the Latino community repay them with the same level of affection and warmth that they have bestowed upon us. Como decía mi Abuelita María: ¡Cuernos!

Finally, this call goes out to anyone who will respond to it: we need more critics. As an executive board member of the National Book Critics Circle, an organization that has been granting career-making awards for the last thirty-six years, I am one of only a handful of Latina/o critics and most of us have served on the twenty-four-member executive board within the last five years.

Literary criticism is a sophisticated community conversation between the writer, the reader, and the critic. It is the evaluation that places the art within various social and cultural contexts, and that engages the power and relevance of a book. We can still have readers and writers without the critic, that's true, but the critic is also an important translator for those who insist on believing that Latina/o writing is lesser than, regional, foreign, and derivative. The only training you need to become a critic is to be a good reader and to develop a critical position: *Do you like the book? Why or why not?* We need the critics writing for blogs, for journals, for newsletters, and literary web sites. We can't only write the books, we need to talk about them. More specifically, we need to read and talk about each others' books. It never ceases to surprise me when I find out that Latina/o writers have not read the books by other Latina/o writers. It's like those people who don't read poetry but write it, and then expect the rest of us to be the readers they are not. What kind of message are we sending to our fellow writers: "You're not worth reading but I am"? What kind of narcissism is that?

The truth is that criticism is one level of literary activism that remains neglected by most of us. It's so easy when we pretend we're "just writers" and not critics. It's so easy when we convince ourselves that it's a whole other genre, better left to the intellectuals and academics who "do that kind of thing." I'll say this: if you are thinking about what you are reading, then you can be a critic. Read more, read better, and you will be a kick-ass critic. We need those voices to speak up in the face of those who will continue to dismiss our literature as lesser than, regional, foreign, and derivative.

Only if this multidimensional effort is made can we thrive as a community of artists and can we begin to celebrate that our bookshelves are expanding and that the number of nationally recognized names is growing. Only then can we hold the ladder for those who are reaching the top and for those who are about to step onto the first important rungs. Only then will numbers have meaning and agency and endurance.

I'd like to close by addressing the participants of this, the National Latino Writers Conference—I like repeating that name because nowhere else does something like this exist, so I want to keep it alive on my tongue and savor the wondrous beauty of it.

Esteemed new members of the Latino writing community, esteemed participants of the National Latino Writers Conference, write and write well. You are artists in a time of crisis, and these conflicts will burden you as much as they will inspire you to move that pen over paper or to press down on those keys on the board. Our veteran writers are dying, our seasoned writers are weary, and the world we live in is not the peaceful, tolerant Eden our immigrant bordercrossers envisioned for us, their descendants. But it is still a world worth fighting for and one of those unflappable weapons we have inherited is language. Each of us here knows the power of literacy: did not that first book you held in your hands initiate a trek that has brought you to the paradise of language? Did not that first childish scribble with pencil or crayon set aflame that dream of authoring an entire book?

Now you must dream bigger dreams and envision possibilities beyond being "just a writer." This country already has plenty of writers, it's *activist writers* who are in short supply and in loud demand as we continue to gain momentum as Latina/o artists and lose ground as Latina/o citizens. These two roles (artist and citizen) are not mutually exclusive, they are perpetually linked, and if one breaks down, the other will collapse right on top of it.

We are now a decade into the new millennium. The plagues of the past have been resurrected, but so too the fury of the antidote. Let us fight our battles with poetry, with theater, with story, and let us lace those words with culture and history. Let us stand our ground over nuestra tierra. *Esta es nuesta tierra*, this is our land. So allow us to remember those who came before, those who wrote it down, and to be remembered by those who will write it down in the next decade of the new millennium. That's how it works—one link locking around another, one branch holding up the next—so that together we remain unbreakable, unshakable.

So keep that in mind as you engage in the power of the word these next few days. This is a life-changing writers conference, but you should expect nothing less from it because it is a Latina/o writers conference. Much is at stake in the teaching and the learning, because much is at stake in the writing. We have made incredible strides as an artist community, but not without sacrifice and certainly not without struggle. Now there will be more sacrifice and more struggle, but take comfort in the company you will keep.

in memoriam, Dr. Hector Torres

The Gay Brown Beret Suite

Note: Professor Don Gagnon, the board representative of the LGBT and popular culture caucuses, invited me to be a featured speaker at the Northeast Modern Language Association's thirtieth anniversary conference in Boston. He had read my memoir *Butterfly Boy* and was particularly interested that I address in my comments the intersection between ethnicity, class, and sexuality. This was familiar territory for me, though I had always approached the nexus through my creative work, not necessarily through a speech. But the more I thought about it, the more I realized how I had been articulating my existence on that plane through the Q & A sessions immediately following my literary readings. Audience members inevitably guided the discussion toward matters of ethnicity, class, and sexuality, but also language, writing process, and the connections between politics and creativity. Thus, I seized the opportunity to provide an honest and charged testimony about my personal journey as a gay Chicano writer, necessarily vocal and sentimental about my convictions as a representative of two distinct (and much-maligned) groups that cross paths within me every time I breathe. I wanted to address the tensions between these two groups (the queer and the Latino) and to affirm that they are inextricable from the fibers of my body. I cannot choose one identity over the other. If anything, writing this speech helped me understand how more alike than different these two groups are, and how much more of a victory it would be if these two communities worked together to attain the dignity, respect, and visibility they both seek. In any case, this was a healthier exercise for me than for anyone else, and all I can ask is that people of any group understand that there is no dilemma here as much as there's a possibility. Solidarity will be the key to survive and thrive in the new millennium. Divide and conquer is an old, but effective strategy. We can succumb and surrender, or we can unite and triumph.

February 28, 2009

Story of my life: moving through different landscapes, speaking different languages, comfortable here, there, and everywhere, yet frequently contending with moments in which one part of my identity is singled out, isolated for the sake of derision (against my sexuality), or exoticization (in response to my ethnicity).

Over the years I have learned to weather these exchanges with some level of understanding, though each encounter costs me varying degrees of frustration and offense. Like the many years I've had to deal with the response to my name. Once people hear it is "Rigoberto," a few well-meaning types will inevitably ask, "Does it mean something in Spanish?"

When I was younger I'd say, "No, it doesn't mean anything." Which of course, is false, since it means I'm Mexican, that I've inherited my father's connection to his Purépecha and Spanish ancestry, and that my parents made the wise decision not to Anglicize my name even though I had been born in the United States all those many years ago.

As I got older and sassier, I'd answer: "It means shit-kicker." Which is true to a certain extent because I've been fighting my way through college and life, adapting and adopting, assimilating and acculturating, pressing my thumb and forefinger around the rosary bead as firmly as I press my thumb and forefinger around the stem of the martini glass.

And if I'm feeling really naughty (and exasperated that I've been split apart once again) I answer (in an effort to bring my identity back to its wholeness): "It means cocksucker."

In any case, when I enter a room it's my ethnic identity that comes in first, my sex and sexual orientation follow, though not very far behind. It's like my African American colleague says: "The first thing people notice is that I'm black. The second thing they notice is that I'm a woman." What she doesn't say is that these two parts of her identity reveal themselves only milliseconds apart, and yet, the political movements that these two parts of her being can espouse couldn't seem farther away from each other. Though notable efforts have been made—and usually by black women themselves—to build bridges between the groups that struggle for racial and gender equality, I can certainly relate to belonging to two groups whose philosophies and histories come across as mutually exclusive.

I turn the mirror on myself and see a Chicano and a gay man. Both are politicized identities. One shaped by the need for community, a communal voice to speak out against the institutional discrimination against Mexican-born citizens and their American-born children. A need for visibility and space, for safety and dignity, and we *will* take to the damn streets if we have to! The other was shaped by the need for community, a communal voice to speak out against the institutional discrimination against American-born citizens. A need for visibility and space, for safety and dignity, and we *will* take to the damn streets if we have to! The overlap is obvious, isn't it? And, yet . . .

If I walk as a gay man into my Chicano community, its shortcomings become apparent—our Catholic roots and history of machismo give way to a discriminatory practice within it. Oh, let me not start on the gay jokes, which are the first jokes we learn as young men to distinguish the healthy lifestyle from the unhealthy one, between normal and desirable masculine behavior from the not-normal, not-masculine, and certainly not-desirable. In our jokes, we not only learn about the effeminate and grotesque gay man, but about gay dogs and gay cars and gay clothes and gay predators who lurk inside our fears, just waiting for a window to open, an opportunity to take advantage, to seduce and corrupt. The gay man is the devil incarnate, except that he doesn't want to enter our hearts, no, he wants to enter a more forbidden place—our pants.

And so I walk into the rally and screech with attitude, swiveling my head, "Chicano power, people!" How well *that* goes over. The presence of a mariposa, a joto, a maricón among straight men, Chicanos, is an invasion, an encroachment, a threat. What is it about straight men anyway that they flatter themselves with the ability to attract members of the same sex? Seriously, vato, some of us queens have standards, or at the very least, eyesight.

Now let me enter the queer space, where we already know what we do and brag about how often and, really, girl, it ain't all about that, because we've got plenty of fight in the rainbow arena—it's all about gay rights and the cure for AIDS, no matter where on the spectrum you set your queer self. But, seriously, the movement has been dominated by gay white men, and white men who are gay don't like to be reminded of white privilege or male privilege because *they're gay*, and gay means subject to ridicule, violence, and oppression, and isn't that en par with other types of discrimination? Perhaps, but I also recognize the Othered position of gay men of color *within* white gay space—how we are exoticized and eroticized: the black stud, the Latin lover, the dark chocolate, the café con leche, the big black dick, the "fuck me in Spanish, papi chulo." I also know that growing up gay means worshipping the white male body—the dominant flesh on pornography, the dominant character in fiction and film, the dominant face on gay magazine covers. *White is beautiful, white is beautiful.* And you, little Mexican boy, are not white. You are *not* white. You are simply gay. You already know what your family thinks about *that.*

And, yet, these two embattled spaces are my spaces, my troubled, complicated, cherished homes. Imperfect, dysfunctional, and sometimes a little intimidating given that the focus is on the repulsion or appeal of one's sexual prowess: one place won't let me in, the other one won't let me out.

I once gave a presentation in an LGBT literature class whose students had read my memoir *Butterfly Boy.* Once the class was dismissed, a young white man rushed up to me and asked: "There's just one thing I don't understand: if it was so difficult to grow up gay in your community, why would you want to go back?"

I gave a quick, impulsive answer: "Because I love my people."

I have had to answer similar curiosities when I make appearances in Chicano Studies classes: "Why do call yourself a gay Chicano writer? Why can't you just call yourself a Chicano writer? Or better yet, why can't you just call yourself a writer and let the work speak for itself?"

Because I love my people, and I celebrate my people, and I claim both my ethnicity and my sexuality in the literary landscape where "just a writer" means universal, and if I were to draw a picture of "just a writer" he would be male, he would be white, he would be straight. Just like it happens in books—the universal male character is white, unless the author points out he's black or Latino or Asian. And he is straight, unless the author points out he's not.

If I feel like being flippant or dismissive I simply say: "I call myself a gay Chicano writer because I *love* accessories!" But if I had the time to pronounce, not only my criticisms, but also my appreciation for the positive elements of my two communities, I'd say:

When I enter Chicano space I swell with pride—the history and culture of a people who work and play and make love beneath the universe with the pre-Columbian tongue—Coatlicue, Huitzilopochtli, Quetzalcoatl—who listen for the guidance of the living and the dead, whose fury and activism is fueled by the fires of Spanish, of familial loyalty, of indigenous nationhood, of a spirituality whose ceremonies are both secular and sacred, biblical and mythological. The legend says that we are brown because we are the children of the sun, heat simmers and boils in our blood depending on our emotion.

We are also the children of the earth, laborers and nurturers, the people who express grief and praise in song, poetry, and prayer—give us a guitar and we will strum you a music that's a combination of all three. Lend us your ear and we will break your heart.

We are the storytellers and the travelers, the healers and the magicians, the bordercrossers who can move through walls, fences, and international lines, with or without permission. This extraordinary legacy inspires my work and pushes me into action when choices like apathy and inaction seem simpler and easier to achieve.

When I enter queer space I swell with pride at the ultimate expression of visibility and fierceness—the forbidden language of intimacy and same-sex touch, affection, and attraction made public and beautiful. The dark rooms where we have been taught to place our desires and fantasies have earned the hard-won light of our queer pioneers: the writers, the librarians, the teachers, the administrators, the politicians, and the lawyers, but also the postal workers, the mechanics, the barbers, the nurses, the factory workers, and the window washers. You can't turn to any profession without one of our faces showing through.

It is in this space where I learned to lose my shame and to welcome the moment of recognition—*ah, so you are as well, how wonderful for the two of us.*

It is in this space where I learned not to feel asexual or abnormal—those convenient closets that explain us to and dismiss us from the heteronormative world. What a lovely act is the act of love when it's not shrouded in secrecy or whispered. And how empowering to enter the room that flowers with the necessary symbols—from the rainbow flag to the pink triangle, the beacons of a safe zone.

I suppose that in the ideal world I wouldn't have to remind Chicanos that issues of sexuality are now part of the concerns to be engaged by our Brown Beret movement in the new millennium; and I wouldn't have to remind gay men that issues of race are now part of the concerns to be engaged by the Pink Beret movement in the new millennium and indeed, bridges are being built, but the burden usually falls on the gay Chicano, on queer men of color in general.

Indeed, this is not, despite Barack Obama in the White House, an ideal world—not yet. And the reminders of the long rocky roads to harmony sadden me.

The Latino vote and its participation in the anti-gay marriage campaign reminded me of shame, not mine but my community's—how immigrants bring with them the marvels of the kitchen and the cruelty of religious values, how the families that I love choose not to love me back. This homophobia took a personal turn for me when I wrote the children's book *Antonio's*

Card, a picture book about a young Latino with two mommies. The book was subsequently banned from various schools and libraries, and my e-mail was (and continues to be) sullied by death threats and insults: *You are garbage! You're disgusting! You make me sick!* (Very unimaginative put-downs, I might add. People need to read more.)

There I was, offering a gift to the same-sex couples who parented and blessed our broken world with kindness, and suddenly, the unkindness from people who were also parents and who couldn't see themselves in the illustrations depicting love and understanding.

I hope that my young adult novels, *The Mariposa Club* series, fare better as they run along to the school of hard knocks, though I suspect these books about four gay high school seniors alarms more than amuses. I wrote the series inspired by the tragedy of Lawrence King, the young gay student from Oxnard, California, who was shot to death by another young man who felt threatened after Lawrence King revealed his crush on him. In 2008, twenty years after I graduated from high school, we're still frightened of the gay kid. If I could wave a magic wand and make this dangerous condition go away, I would, but all I've got is a sharp pencil and a muscle on the forefinger that's ready to flex. And so I flex, adding to my grief and my resolve the deaths of Carl Walker-Hoover, Jaheem Herrera, and countless others.

My contributions to the cause have been literary because I'm a writer, that's my chosen path. So it hurts me when my labor is chastised or lessened. When I was first starting out, writing and publishing my early poems and stories, I overheard a veteran writer say to another, "That Rigoberto, he's a promising young writer, but too bad he's gay." That "too bad he's gay" has haunted me ever since, and at night I can hear it beating like a pulse in the dark, and sometimes it keeps me awake because it reminds me of the times when I tried to hide my gay skin beneath my brown one, and how that deception during my fragile adolescence nearly pushed me to suicide. Yes, suicide, the ultimate "I'm sorry I was born this way."

And though I find more tolerance and acceptance as a Chicano writer in the queer community, the dismal representation of gay Latino/Chicano writers in queer-themed anthologies and conference panels makes it difficult for me not to feel like a token when I'm constantly the only one or one of a few represented. And if I express my discontent I get this answer: "But we try to reach out and we get very little response from Latinos." Oh, girl! It's what white heterosexuals have been saying all along as excuses and explanations for the dearth of Latino representation in publishing. Now I have to hear it from my girlfriends in struggle as well?

Despite those affronts, I continue doing what I set out to do, perform activism with ink—writing it down so that my words remain in print long after my voice falls silent. With my poetry, my stories, my essays, and even my children's books and books for young adults, I am not going away easily, and with each book I'm making it harder and harder to be ignored. I am brown, I am queer, here I write, here I am.

All I have to do to give myself some sunlight during the dark times is to look south of the border—if the anxieties in Latin America can be assuaged, then anxieties can be assuaged anywhere. A bit overdue but more than gestures of equality all the same: In 1998, Ecuador's new constitution introduced protections against discrimination based on sexual orientation. In 1999, Chile decriminalized same-sex intercourse. In 2000, Rio de Janeiro's state legislature banned sexual-orientation discrimination in public and private establishments. In 2002, Buenos Aires guaranteed all couples, regardless of gender, the right to register civil unions. In 2003, México passed a federal anti-discrimination law that included sexual orientation. In 2004, the government of Brazil initiated a program with nongovernmental organizations to change social attitudes toward sexuality. In 2006, Mexico City approved the Societal Cohabitation Law, granting same-sex couples marital rights identical to those for common-law relationships between a man and a woman. In 2007, Uruguay passed a law granting access to health benefits, inheritance, parenting, and pension rights to all couples who have cohabited for at least five years. In 2008, Nicaragua reformed its penal code to decriminalize same-sex relations. And same-sex marriage will soon be legal in Argentina. Now I'm holding my breath for my own home, the United States of America—for the entire country to come to its senses, not just pockets of liberal triumphs one blue state at a time.

Funny, isn't it, how a country that flaunts its freedoms and its democratic process can be so selective about whom those freedoms and that process serves? In our beloved country, the two groups that seem to be constantly under governmental siege are my two communities: my Mexican family and my queer family. Sometimes I wonder why I haven't been deported and gay bashed at the same time, me, the queer son of "illegal immigrants."

I suppose this is the part where I should own up to my self-designated label as a Gay Brown Beret and call into tough-cookie question this hatred for the Mexican, this hatred for the queer, and sadly, I have plenty of personal experience to draw from: from being called a wetback when I was a professor in Illinois, to being called a faggot when I was a visiting writer in Arizona, from watching my mother afraid to go to work when the INS (now ICE) started raiding the packinghouses, to shaking hands with instead of kissing my lover when we said our good-byes at the airport, from freaking out that I would lose my student loan with the approval of California's Proposition 187 (another anti-immigrant law), to being picketed at one of my readings of *Antonio's Card,* from getting pulled over by the immigration officer when I was driving back to college, to getting denied service at a restaurant on the Mexican side of the border because they "didn't serve people like me."

If anything, these victimizations have taught me not to surrender to the role of victim, but to rise to the call to action—to protest and speak out. In the beginning the fire was similar to the one that politicizes many young people and so I signed up for the rally, the sit-in, the march, the petitioning, and the vote-getting. Oh, sure, the body was more resilient and energetic during the college years, and I could stay up all night making protest signs and then stand on my feet for hours the following day, on no sleep. But those hard-core days are limited, and when I knew I could reach larger numbers through my writing, the decision to stay behind and sit in front of the computer was a logical one.

What many people don't know is how solitary this form of activism is. In fact, I would say that it's lonely, the sitting down and sipping on cold coffee when the only other voice in the office is that little beep on AOL that lets you know you just received a new message in your inbox and then what a heartbreak when it turns out it's a spam announcement letting you know your e-mail address just won the Irish lottery. But it's a necessary effort. How else will the idea of a better world survive?

Survival, is that what I call this key-stroking in the early hours of the morning, in the later hours of the night? I must, I have no other method of dealing with the shitty news that comes my way: just recently I was told that my column in *The El Paso Times* is going to shut down after ten years of reviewing exclusively books by Latino writers because the features editor (my long-time champion) is retiring; just recently my best friend in Albuquerque called me, distraught that the Senate in New Mexico rejected a bill that would allow domestic partnerships because it was "marriage in disguise"; just recently I heard back from my young cousins who have been in hiding in Texas for months after their parents, my aunt and my uncle, were deported.

The human in me, the advocate, the friend, the cousin in me, sat down and cried because I'm entitled to the visceral grief that can overwhelm even an iron butterfly like me. I always thought that having two communities doubled my chances of a date on a Saturday night, that being in the middle was akin to playing the role of the Lucky Pierre in a ménage a trois, but in reality, getting fucked by both sides is not a pleasant experience at all.

But then, when the tears evaporate and the crumpled tissue papers look more like daisies than knots of Kleenex stiffened by dried mucus, when the screen tires of deaf blankness and thirsts for interaction, I turn on the computer and open the files that run on the double-fight, not the double-fuck that is my birthright.

Indeed I am hopeful. My hope lies in the perseverance of my disparate communities that have yet to march in step, but that are marching forward nonetheless. I'd like to believe that people like me, representatives of the double identity, double indemnity, are up front raising the baton, but I'm much too modest for such a proclamation. I'd rather say I'm part of the band, fourth or fifth row, just another vato, just another girl, sticking her neck out trying to make the group shot for the yearbook. Isn't that what matters in the end? Not what you do, but what you did?

It sounds odd speaking of myself and my experiences as if I were reaching the end of a life or an era—after all I am still going strong, relatively healthy, relatively happy with a tenured appointment at a state university, and—as of this year—a sorta boyfriend (yes, mami, the candles and daily prayers to San Lázaro do work!); but one thing I've learned is not to let the comforts trick me into complacency, because it's not about me but about something bigger than me.

Last year I was engaged in a teleconference with the board members of a prestigious poetry organization. I pointed out—yet again—that this organization's efforts at addressing diversity were uninspired at best, that white liberal guilt becomes so easily soothed with the inclusion of one or two African American poets into their season's programming: *What about Latino poets? Our population is only 50 million or so. What about Chicanos? We are only two-thirds of that US Latino population?*

I was met with silence, and then, one of the head honchos said to me: "I don't understand, Rigoberto. The poetry world has been so good to you, publishing you and giving you awards. Why do you keep complaining? Why don't you just let it go and enjoy the fruits of your labor?"

That comment reminded me of the earnest young man I spoke about earlier, the one who came up to me when I visited the LGBT literature class: such ignorance disguised as innocence, such refusal to recognize the activist who doesn't carry the picket sign or chant the protest songs, but who acts out of communal duty nonetheless. I do it because I love my people. I speak up, I act up, I stand up, because I love my people. I write because I love my people.

I am not embarrassed by the sentimentality of these proclamations, I am empowered by them. Therefore my politics cannot be a costume—certainly I couldn't sustain such a theater—especially during these times of economic hardship in which the arts and literature are under assault and dismissed as luxuries. This is probably the time we need it the most—we are suffering such terrible losses already, let us not lose the right to imagine, to express, and to address.

My name is Rigoberto González, and I am a gay Brown Beret—I've got a mouth, an attitude, and many languages. I've got much work yet to do and plenty left to say.

Trinity

Toward a Mariposa Consciousness

> May we strive always for illegitimacy and unlawfulness in this criminal culture. May our thoughts and actions remain illicit. May we continue to make art that incites censorship and threatens to bring the army beating down our desert door.
>
> —*Cherríe L. Moraga*

1. Butterfly (A)jar

Chew with your mouth open. No, this isn't an affront to Mami's lessons on table manners because even though it's her rule she didn't come up with it. Neither did she invent such maxims as "boys don't cry" and "boys don't play with dolls." It is no more her fault than it is yours to have been born a boy with a prescription attached to your sex organs. What are you then, if anatomically you are male, like your fathers and uncles, but your interests and behavior don't always match theirs? It seems like everyone in the family is complicit in policing your mannerisms, your way of speaking, your means of expressing pain or surprise. Those small no-no's, publicly decried, make you think every move you make has the potential to become a crisis. Oh, yes, everyone brings a piece of wood to your coffin, what society calls "a closet" so that no one gets indicted for burying a breathing child.

How can you blame those well-meaning people for wanting to protect you from harm? Jotos and maricones are but caricatures of femininity and though they're always invited to the family gatherings (through jokes and stories), they're only there to be ridiculed and then they fade away, wispy as smoke, with the laughter. You giggle too, comfortable in your knowledge that it isn't you in the narrative, even when more than one person in the room glances furtively in your direction. Silly, silly boy. Each joto joke is a message, a warning, another pinche coffin nail you hold between your forefinger and thumb as the hammer strikes.

There's no mystery about how you learn the art of shame. The lessons begin with simple directives like *Don't chew with your mouth open.* Eventually they grow into more complicated instruction with subtext you will not understand until many years later, like: *Don't cross your legs when you sit* and *Don't spend all your time with girls.* And there are those lessons you learn the hard way, like *Don't practice your cheerleader kicks while Papi's watching the game.* The dishrags you use for pom-poms are just another stroke of creativity your parents don't appreciate, and when your father beats you with a can of beer during half-time, it's for your own good. "You should be grateful," Mami says, wiping your tears away with the pom-poms. "He let you live. He could have killed you." So the next time you sit next to your father during the football game, you wear a pair of butt-tight little shorts—*in your head*—and you kick higher than any of those skinny white girls on the field. Imagination as recourse, as survival in mariposa life. Without it, you are truly dead.

Hidden away or hiding in plain sight (that's easy to do when those you embarrass keep wishing you invisible), it's no wonder you gravitate toward those tools that stimulate your brain: books, for example, and magazines that allow you to ogle at the pictures of grown men posing like Samson between columns of text. (Don't worry, no one's telling.) Your bookworm ways protect you; in the Latino household, the act of literacy is an act of respect. And so you read in peace about war, violence, heartbreak, death, struggle, love, lust, sex, salvation, redemption, and every other configuration of emotion, expression, and desire that allows you to envision your eventual emancipation. No one fucks with the reader.

Although sometimes reading does fuck with *you.* You read on the Internet and in pop culture magazines how times have changed for the homosexual—gay marriage, gay adoption, hate crime legislation, socially acceptable role models such as Ellen and the singing gay kid from *Glee*—and this gives you comfort somehow though deep down you know that that's not the place you're currently in. You're still a citizen of a small planet, all the more suffocating as you sit cocooned to the corners of the house watching everyone else watching you. Yet you must revel in the fact that none of them can read your mind, your mariposa inner world. Even when you chew with your mouth closed you know you're chewing with your mouth wide open.

You bide your time, you're industrious in your word-gathering, your strength-building, your wood-splitting—the older you become the more control you have over your future, indeed your destiny. The catalog of humiliations, reprimands, and shamings will be the shell of your yesterdays you step out of like a body-cast, and its ghost will help you define your tomorrows.

The lights are out, the room is dark. Mami's radio lowers its voice in the kitchen and Papi's coffee cup chimes in on occasion. In the stillness, in the quiet you have space to dream and fantasize. If tears come to visit you again, they will come big with hope this time. High school is almost over and your days in this house are numbered. From the kitchen comes a murmur too soft to understand but you know it's an affectionate exchange between the people who have caused you such pain and who you love nonetheless. The pang of loss overcomes you suddenly and for a moment you wonder if you should stay instead. But just as quickly you resolve to love your parents from a distance. Besides, they never really leave you; there's enough room in your head for your parents, your home, and your neighborhood to come with you wherever you go. You leave *them* because you want to thrive.

The sky is full of clouds and you search for the moon like a mouth. You will press against it like a kiss good-bye.

2. Mariposa Lit

A study of the new generation of gay Chicano/Latino literature written by authors who received their college education in the 1990s and beyond has yet to receive serious consideration. I use that decade as a demarcation because during this period, the previous generation of gay Chicano/Latino writers was actively publishing and shaping via a literary mentorship the *next* generation of writers. I have mentioned a few of these jotoranos before (Arturo Islas, John Rechy, Michael Nava, Richard Rodriguez, Francisco X. Alarcón) and I'd add to that list the Chicano writers Gil Cuadros and Luis Alfaro, the Colombian writer Jaime Manrique, the Cuban American writers Ernesto Mestre and Rafael Campo, and the Puerto Rican poets Rane Arroyo and Miguel Algarín. The *next* generation came of age as college students during the rise of the Internet, in the era when LGBT writers had institutional community and visibility through organizations such as the Lambda Literary Foundation, with its focus on literary programming, and The Publishing Triangle, an association of lesbians and gay men in publishing, when academic programs and conferences, scholarly and literary, were beginning to embrace if not recognize the burgeoning field of gay and lesbian studies, gender studies, and critical sexualities, when queer pioneers and trailblazers were being honored as exemplary artists and activists, their life stories and bibliographies disseminated publicly as shining examples of citizenship and artistry. Though there was some resistance within academia to the "queering" of American letters and intellectuals of color continued to point out the shortcomings of a growing discipline that didn't properly address issues of race, there were now various arenas to engage in debate and dialogue. In short, imperfect as it was, queer lit became more available and teachable than ever before. This privileged education and flourishing landscape allowed young gay Chicano/Latino writers-in-the-making to demand a more specific, ethnic- and gender-identified queer history, queer literary ancestry, and indeed queer legacy, even as they positioned themselves in solidarity to lesbian writers of color (who were much more proactive and successful in those endeavors) and to the queer writing community at large. The act of building a gay Chicano/Latino consciousness is not an act of separatism, but an act of self-preservation. To that end, I will call this next generation of gay Chicano/Latino writing "mariposa lit."

In 1999, two important anthologies were published that heralded from opposite coasts though fortified by similar ideologies: *Bésame Mucho: New Gay Latino Fiction*, edited by Jaime Manrique in New York City, and *Virgins, Guerrillas, and Locas: Gay Latinos Writing about Love*, edited by Jaime Cortez in Berkeley. These projects bridged seasoned writers to up-and-coming voices, ushering in a critical mass that took flight as a pan-Latino multigenerational coalition because of the small number of Chicano/Latino writers who self-identified as gay. Up to this point gay Chicano/Latino writers had appeared in queer anthologies that were predominantly white—their work, nuanced by a Chicano/Latino cultural context, remained isolated within the pages of queer-identity politics. Although it was always a pleasant surprise to stumble upon a gay Latino piece of writing, that unexpected reward began to feel like a false gesture toward diversity akin to tokenism. (To keep it fair, I must clarify that the gay presence in Chicano/Latino anthologies was just as rare if not entirely absent.) With the publication of *Bésame Mucho* and *Virgins, Guerrillas, and Locas*, a writing community situated within an ethnic as well as a queer political position was formally announced. Since then, however, there have been only a handful of projects that can supplement these two groundbreaking books. Among them, *Queer Codex: Rooted* (2005) and *Joto: An Anthology of Queer Xicano Poetry* (2012), Chicano/Latino poetry edited by Lorenzo Herrera y Lozano; *Mariposas: A Modern Anthology of Queer Latino Poetry* (2008), edited by Emanuel Xavier; *From Machos to Mariposas: New Gay Latino Fiction* (2011), edited by Charles Rice-González and Charlie Vásquez; and *Ambientes: New Queer Latino Writing* (2011), edited by Lázaro Lima and Felice Picano.

Note that *mariposa* as a queer Latino term has been featured prominently in projects showcasing a gay Chicano/Latino identity, hence my naming this period of literary production "mariposa lit." I will add to that list my own works, *Butterfly Boy: Memories of a Chicano Mariposa* (2006) and my young adult novel trilogy *The Mariposa Club* (2009), *Mariposa Gown* (2012), and *Mariposa U.* (2014). Though it is a word that traces a specific lineage to Mexican slang and therefore more commonly engaged by gay Chicano writers, "mariposa" has grown in popularity and sentimental significance, an expansion of queer nomenclature that now addresses queer Latinos in general. Incidentally, the editors of the two mariposa anthologies mentioned above are multi-ethnic: Puerto Rican Ecuadorean (Xavier), black Puerto Rican (Rice-González), and Puerto Rican Cuban (Vásquez).

Mariposa may come across as an obvious symbol or image with the caterpillar-to-butterfly transformation paralleling a young man's coming out of the closet/cocoon, but the trope can be articulated through a more emotionally charged language: the transformation is actually a transition. From one creature is born a different living being that bears the memory of its past life in its genes—the past is neither erased nor abandoned; the freedom of inhabiting a second manifestation of the self also represents a second chance at life; the use of the Spanish word for "butterfly" gestures toward the Chicano/Latino ancestral tongue, but also to the hurtful legacy of name-calling—by taking back the word (the way the word "queer" has been repositioned within a positive identity-building discourse) gay Chicanos/Latinos claim and redirect its power. There is an inclination to idealize coming out as the ultimate avenue toward happiness (the transition from caterpillar to butterfly also signifies a transition from weakness to fierceness), and although coming out has allowed young men to envision themselves as part of an alternative, less oppressive narrative, coming out is not the end of the journey, nor is this state of liberation removed from other risks, dangers, conflicts, or crises. But neither is it completely fraught with anxiety, trauma, grief, and homophobia—all those negative elements those who are not gay (our families, our religious leaders, for example) warned us about. The mariposa experience is complex: it is an individual experience but it is speckled with familiar events, conversations, obstacles, and triumphs that allow us to be as human—visible and fallible—as everyone else, especially our mariposa readers.

Mariposa lit does not function as a formula, although its heartbeat is the intersection of race/ethnicity, class, and sexuality. Most of the writers of this movement come from working-class backgrounds, are the sons of immigrants, and are the first to pursue a college education or leave home. For prose writers, the hard-won passage to freedom, which sometimes leads to other forms of distress, is negotiated in a number of their fictional narratives as one thread out of many. That proves true in such works as Emanuel Xavier's *Christ-Like* (1999), an autobiographical novel detailing the journey of a disowned son from street hustler to empowered member of an outsider community of drag queens and other queer performance artists; in Erasmo Guerra's *Between Dances* (2000), which charts the secret lives of young gay men who escape their small towns and find themselves struggling for orientation in the big city as go-go boys; in H. G. Carrillo's *Loosing My Espanish* (2004) a young gay Afro-Cuban history teacher who has worked hard to assimilate—despite his many markers of difference—when suddenly he finds himself reassessing his entire life to locate the moment he made a wrong turn and ended up a disenfranchised person anyway; and in Erik Orrantia's *Normal Miguel* (2010) another young gay teacher flees his Mexican privileged-but-stifling middle-class comforts in the big city to find community and purpose in a rural school for indigenous children.

As in a number of heterosexual Chicano/Latino narratives, the young protagonist continues to occupy an important place in mariposa lit, where the battles at home and community include the struggles of coming of age while coming out, and reconciling the limitations that come with being a disempowered underage dependent. The young gay protagonists in the story collections by Manuel Muñoz, *Zigzagger* (2003) and *The Faith Healer of Olive Avenue* (2007) must contend with a troubled present and an uncertain future; at least two queer characters inhabit Alex Espinoza's debut novel, *Still Water Saints* (2007); Charles Rice-González's novel *Chulito* (2011) features a street-wise kid who finds a place for himself in his tough Bronx neighborhood after he falls in love with another young man; and in Justin Torres's novel *We the Animals* (2011), a part white, part Puerto Rican boy heads into adolescence suddenly aware that he's much different from the two older brothers he thought were indistinguishable from him.

Poetry, though an entirely different genre, also offers an opportunity to explore and express mariposa experience, observation, and imagination through narrative and lyrical language. Like the prose writers, most of the following poets come from working-class backgrounds, are the sons of immigrants, and are the first to pursue a college education or leave home. An important exception is Emanuel Xavier, whose rise to literary acclaim was not aided by a formal education, but by his popularity as a New York City spoken word artist and the compelling journey of his life. Indeed, if mariposa lit can identify its beginning, it might be found in Xavier's self-published poetry collection *Pier Queen* (1997). He continued to build on his body of work as he matured into a more polished poet with *Americano* (2002) and *If Jesus Were Gay* (2010).

Notable among the published books of poetry are Miguel Murphy's *A Book Called Rats* (2003), with its poetics of danger and violence communicated through a distinctly homoerotic imagery; Lorenzo Herrera y Lozano's *Santo de la Pata Alzada* (2005), which pays homage, like Xavier's *Christ-Like*, to a life-saving path via a community of cross-dressers and other queer outsiders, as well as to his bilingual Texas environment; Steven Cordova's *Long Distance* (2009), which places at its center a speaker who is HIV positive; Richard Blanco's *Looking for the Gulf Hotel* (2012), which is the third collection for the gay Cuban exile but the first to sustain a focus on his sexuality; and finally, Eduardo C. Corral's *Slow Lightning* (2012), the Arizona native's love letter to his literary ancestors and the troubled legacy of his desert landscape through the queering of the US–México border.

I must also mention two poets who are identified as gay Latinos (though not necessarily by them) and whose poetry doesn't always reflect the concerns extrapolated in the category of mariposa lit. Instead, these poets (Urayoán Noel, of Puerto Rican descent, and Roberto Tejada, of Mexican descent) exercise a vastly different aesthetic, that of experimental and avant-garde poetics, a political postmodernist position that challenges convenient categories, agendas, or labels—a queer identity in itself.

It is important to note that although my focus here is published literature, a mariposa consciousness is palpable on the stage through spoken word and theatrical productions, much of which is not readily available in print, such as the work of Chicano playwrights Ricardo Bracho and Carlos Manuel and the Chilean American playwright Guillermo Reyes (who is slightly older but merits inclusion here, particularly because of the recent release of his memoir *Madre & I: A Memoir of Our Immigrant Lives* published in 2010). Additionally, the Texas-based performance troupe Tragic Bitches (made up of long-time members Lorenzo Herrera y Lozano, Dino Foxx, and Adelina Anthony) has gathered some of its provocative material in *Tragic Bitches: An Experiment in Queer Xicana & Xicano Performance Poetry* (2011). And if I can add a latent mariposa to the shimmering branch, I will include *Aristotle and Dante Discover the Secrets of the Universe* (2012), a gay love story by veteran Chicano writer (now a jotorano) Benjamin Alire Sáenz, whose exit from the closet was a long time coming.

What I have provided here is at its simplest an introductory reading list and an invitation to seek out those works that act as a compass toward a point of understanding how a new generation of gay Chicano/Latino writers intersect and diverge from the previous generation. Indeed it is heartening to see how the literature is prospering in both independent and mainstream presses with such a small membership, and how mariposa lit is a continuation of and not in contention with the crucial library many of us were exposed to during our formative years. At its most compelling, I have given this generation attention that it has yet to receive even from the next generation of mariposa scholars—the developers of jotería studies—who are researching important avenues of thought, though little in the form of literary criticism. To that end, I was thrilled to discover that the first serious treatment of the field, *Gay Latino Studies: A Critical Reader* edited by Michael Hames-García and Ernesto Javier Martínez, was finally released in 2011. Indeed another milestone toward shaping the critical bookshelf that Chicana/Latina lesbians have been expanding for decades.

I expect that further study by trained scholars will enlighten and educate in ways I have not accomplished using only my writer's eye and my book critic's familiarity with queer Latino writings. The value of mariposa lit is in its activism—each story, essay, poem, or play is placing our queer lives in more varied and complex spaces. No longer can we allow the joto joke and hurtful homophobic language to define or express who we are. Neither should we stop writing the coming-out story or those odes to gay love and gay sex, or stop re-enacting the scripts of our heartaches with our families and lovers, our everyday queer dramas should be performed front and center because these journeys are still our reality. Our confessions, mischief, desires, and behaviors, which disconcert many, should keep doing so—if we sanitize, compromise, or self-censor, we are only pulling out our wings.

3. Mariposa Prayer

Que viva la jotería, the cluster of mariposas at academic conferences who carry power points in their flash-drives tucked neatly into man-purses (from Tumi messenger bags to morrales bought wholesale at the Olveras Street tianguis);

bless the old-school jotoranos who still remember breaking up fights with Mexican drag queens at Esta Noche, back in the day when la Misión had street cred and the stretch marks to prove it;

bless the queer Xicanitos who by middle school outgrow their claustrophobic hometowns like Thermal, El Monte, Madera, Del Río, Casa Grande, and Española, wearing skinny pants with chanclas and dying their hair green to attend the MEChA meetings;

bless the scholarship and fellowship and second job and student loan that saved their mariposa nalgas by lighting a path all the way to the college registration building;

bless the maricón behind the help desk, mariposa putting in his work-study hours, who sees each of his kind coming in wide-eyed and mensa through the front door and so he tilts his head and smiles;

bless the lady at financial aid who looks like our tía Ernestina in her big flowery dress and gorgeous penmanship, and the whole time she's helping us fill out those forms we expect her to lower her voice and ask us, *How's your mami doing, mijo?*;

bless the dorm with its laughter and the Chicana from La Jolla who busts open a can of menudo on Sunday mornings, the library with its whispers, its answers, its glory holes, and its reading table beneath the unflattering fluorescent light from where we take clandestine glimpses at the male crotch parade;

bless the vending machine, the taco truck, the cheap ethnic eats at the student union and the fake blonde MTF who can tap the cash register's buttons with killer press-on nails;

bless the cute college boys who feed our fantasies and las mujeres fuertes who speak up in class to tell the dumb kid in the back to *cut that xenophobic/homophobic/racist/sexist/anti-woman shit up!*;

bless the adjunct who, overworked and underpaid, keeps late office hours to listen to a stressed mariposita start to weep because in high school he had a 4.0 and English was his favorite subject and now he's failing composition;

bless you, adjunct, for your sage advice/patience/kindness even though the stack of uncorrected student papers on the corner of the desk has grown a foot since the kid came in, but thank you, thank you for your bracelet of Catholic saints around the wrist, for pointing north to the tutoring center, for pointing south to the academic adviser, for pointing east to the counseling center, for pointing west to the nicer chair in the office because it's important to be comfortable when getting a crash course on the fundamentals of a compare-and-contrast essay;

bless the queenita from Eastlos who wears a Frida Kahlo T-shirt, a Guadalupe tattoo, and a pierced eyebrow, and who says things like *qué fabulous, qué fierce, qué cabrón* at each comadre hour at the local coffee shop where everyone sweetens their nonfat latté with chisme, noticias, and book reports;

bless the beso, the blowjob, the break-up, the text message from across campus letting you know your future ex-boyfriend is in the language lab;

bless the study groups on e-mail list-servs, the e-vites to the end-of-finals parties, the summer job postings on the cyber bulletin boards, the instant message drama and all-nighter Facebook exchanges about graduate school, martini lounges, CD-ROMs, CDs, STDs, and OTCs;

bless the transsexual speaker at Pride Week, the Chicano trio at Band Week, the queer symposium, the raza colloquium, the scholars and thinkers and writers, purveyors of mariposa lit construction and mariposa theory deconstruction, who show up wearing everything from guayaberas to dirty jeans to Armani suits, a speech/presentation/lecture/reading shining on their teeth like glitter that will stick to every person in the room;

and bless the moment of inspiration when a mariposa graduate student decides to become a mariposa college professor, when a mariposa undergraduate decides to apply for graduate school, when a mariposa school boy looks up at the glow-in-the-dark stars pasted to the ceiling and thinks *Chale, I want the real ones,* and then Googles college entrance requirements until five in the morning—bless all of them, for they shall inherit both heaven and earth.

About the Author

Rigoberto González is the author of thirteen books of poetry and prose, and the editor of *Camino del Sol: Fifteen Years of Latina and Latino Writing.* He is the recipient of Guggenheim and National Endowment of the Arts fellowships, winner of the American Book Award, The Poetry Center Book Award, and The Shelley Memorial Award of The Poetry Society of America, and a grant from the New York Foundation for the Arts. He is contributing editor for *Poets & Writers Magazine*, on the executive board of directors of the National Book Critics Circle, and is associate professor of English at Rutgers-Newark, the State University of New Jersey.